Creative
Change

WHY WE RESIST IT . . .

Creative Change

HOW WE CAN EMBRACE IT

Jennifer Mueller, Ph.D.

HOUGHTON MIFFLIN HARCOURT   BOSTON • NEW YORK   2017

For information about permission to reproduce selections from
this book, write to trade.permissions@hmhco.com or to Permissions,
Houghton Mifflin Harcourt Publishing Company, 3 Park Avenue,
19th Floor, New York, New York 10016.

www.hmhco.com

Library of Congress Cataloging-in-Publication Data
Names: Mueller, Jennifer, date, author.
Title: Creative change : why we resist it ... how we can embrace it /
Jennifer Mueller.
Description: Boston : Houghton Mifflin Harcourt, [2017] |
Includes bibliographical references and index.
Identifiers: LCCN 2016036403 | ISBN 9780544703094 (hardcover) |
Subjects: LCSH: Creative ability in business. | Creative thinking. |
Change (Psychology)
Classification: LCC HD53 .M84 2017 | DDC 658.4/094 — dc23
LC record available at https://lccn.loc.gov/2016036403

Book design by Chrissy Kurpeski
Typeset in Times Ten, Museo, & Museo Sans

Illustration on page 5 courtesy of Katharine Mueller

Printed in the United States of America
DOC 10 9 8 7 6 5 4 3 2 1

FOR STEVEN

Contents

Preface:
The Seeds of Our
Uncreative Destruction

IN 2016, A GROUP OF EMINENT SCIENTISTS —
the Science and Security Board of the *Bulletin of the Atomic Scientists* — including several Nobel laureates, rated our current global predicament as being three minutes to midnight. This means that, according to the smartest people on the planet, the human race is about as close to annihilation as we were during the Cold War, a time when a nuclear war with the Soviet Union seemed like a distinct possibility.

To echo scientist and best-selling author Carl Sagan, humans may not survive our technological adolescence. We have serious problems to solve: global warming, terrorism, pollution, nuclear threats, and more . . . And we need solutions. *Tick tock.*

How do we find solutions? *Creativity.*

We believe creativity will save us. Scientists bet on creativity to save our species. And scientists aren't the only ones who care about creativity. If you are a businessperson, no matter what company you work for, no matter what your industry might be, you will pray for creativity if your company starts to falter and your job is threatened. If you are an entrepreneur, you pray for creativity every day. If you are in the military, creativity is just about the only thing that will help you win a losing battle. If you are an educator, you hope to teach your students to be more creative so that they can solve the complex problems we face, or at least so they can compete in the world.

I believe this eternal hope for what creativity can do for us is part of the reason behind our fascination with creativity and our endless love of it. Most cultures associate creativity with all things good (e.g., joy, beauty, the divine). So the advice has always been to generate more creative ideas! The more ideas we generate, the better, because the sooner we generate the right idea, the sooner we will be able to solve our most pressing problems. Right?

And we have been following this advice. We have been generating lots of ideas. In fact, we know a lot about how to generate creative ideas. With minimal instruction, any student can generate several good ideas in an hour. With a crowdsourcing website, you could potentially generate thousands of ideas in minutes.

So what is holding us back from a better world? As a species, why are we on the existential brink of annihilation? Why are people and corporations and communities and nations still struggling to be creative?

In the case of companies, you might think that they are not doing enough. True and unique creativity is very rare! So perhaps to find that one creative solution that solves our problems, we need to generate many more. Invest in more inspirational idea-generation programs and brainstorming initiatives for groups. Increase your R&D budget. Empower your employees to generate more ideas faster. Take your people on brainstorming retreats and buy brainstorming software.

For nearly twenty years I've devoted my professional life to studying creativity. This dialogue around generating more and more-creative solutions is starting to scare me. That's because my work shows that this dialogue is addressing the wrong problem — a problem we may no longer have. From where I'm sitting, I'm not at all convinced that if someone generates the idea that has the potential to save us all, or to save your company, that it will matter for our society, or for your business.

I'm writing this book to disrupt the dialogue we've been having around the concept of creativity. We need to change this dialogue, and we need to change it fast. Why, you might ask? What problem are we trying to solve? Both good questions. This book is dedicated to answering them.

Here's the problem in a nutshell: I think we have developed lots of great methods to help us generate new ideas and solutions. The problem is, however, that our ability to recognize and to embrace creative solutions is, to put it mildly, dysfunctional. The sad irony is that we are more likely to reject an idea *because* it is creative than to embrace it. If our ability to generate creative ideas far outpaces our ability to truly embrace them, then it doesn't matter if you generate a lot of ideas, because they won't make any impact. Great ideas will be left in the file drawer unimplemented. The solutions that can save us won't have a chance to develop and thrive even though someone, somewhere, took the time and effort to generate them.

In short, right now in our timeline, our problem isn't the idea-generation part of creativity. Our problem is our inexplicable inability to get out of our own way, to disrupt our unproductive thinking, and to embrace the new and the bold. You may have heard of "creative destruction," a term that economist Joseph Schumpeter coined to describe how new technologies can destroy old markets. Well, I'm suggesting that the choice not to embrace creativity will result in another kind of destruction — *uncreative* destruction — sticking to the status quo when urgent and pressing problems require that we embrace creativity immediately.

You might say, "Yes, yes, yes, we already know this. We already know that people resist change." To which I will counter, "Yes, you are right. And if that's true, now do you see the irony around our spending so much time and effort generating the very kinds of ideas we are most likely to reject?"

My colleagues and I believe we can explain this curious puzzle — why we desire creativity so very much, but usually reject it in the end. My goal in the pages that follow is to unveil our best thinking for you about the underlying cause of this hidden barrier.

Here's the good news: We are three whole minutes from midnight, not two and not one. It isn't too late. But it is time to disrupt the dialogue.

Creativity is not magic; I believe we can engineer how we create creativity. And in fact, there are many terrific books and resources to help you generate creative ideas. But this book is not one of them.

Rather, this book contains solutions for how we can embrace creativity, which is a vital process that is, oddly, not often discussed or even acknowledged. I believe that we can *engineer* our ability to embrace creative change. Once we enhance our tendency to embrace the new, then generating lots of ideas will make sense again, because they will have a fair shot at making impact.

To start, you might ask, aren't creative ideas new but also useful? If so, why would people reject them? Chapters 1, 2, and 3 describe the scope and scale of the problem.

Specifically, Chapter 1 defines creative change and unveils what I will call *the hidden innovation barrier* to explain why companies can desire creativity, generate many creative ideas, but still undergo uncreative destruction. In doing so, Chapter 1 asks a surprising question: we know that people love creativity, but could they also *hate* it?

Chapter 2 describes how our hatred of creativity is not a given but is driven by the situations we are in and the resulting mindsets we use (and have been trained to use) when evaluating ideas. This chapter identifies how our mindsets can turn our love and hate of creative ideas on and off.

Chapter 3 delves into the science behind why we hate creativity and the role our mindsets (and expertise) can play. That chapter raises the possibility that a dislike of creativity is something that people will not easily admit. Instead, it is more like a knee-jerk reaction that may operate beneath our conscious awareness.

Chapter 4 provides you with a four-step process and a lifeline to help you self-disrupt your maladaptive mindsets and more accurately see value in creative ideas. This chapter explores how some of the world's most brilliant minds and inventors evaluate creative ideas and aims to provide you with strategies to manage your own negative knee-jerk reactions to reject them.

Chapter 5 flips the coin, providing you with strategies to help others disrupt their thinking and see value in creative ideas. Because creative ideas have unique properties, some influence strategies can backfire and harm your ability to effectively sell them. To combat this, I'll present the FAB framework: fit, aha, and broaden. The FAB framework is built specifically to help you cogently influence others to like and to use creative ideas.

Chapter 6 discusses creative changes in your own organization and raises a controversial and troubling question: Could the very fabric of how most organizations (universities, companies, institutions, governments) are structured in our current day and age evoke a real aversion for creativity — even when we say we desire it? If so, how can we overcome our situational and institutional dislikes? This chapter offers several solutions to help you structure your organization to actively promote, rather than inadvertently deter, creative change.

Chapter 7 spearheads our difficulty recognizing true creative leadership. This could explain the looming "creativity crisis" — research shows that millennials scored lower on creativity tests than prior generations, and modern-day leaders who make it to the top may lack creative-thinking skills. This chapter suggests that the cause of both problems could be linked, and it provides solutions to help us avert this impending community crisis and recognize true creative leadership.

Chapter 8 issues a call to action: stop generating so many solutions and start making creative change. Just about every book on creativity will tell you to generate more solutions, because more is better than fewer. But is it? What if generating more solutions could actually make it *harder* for organizations to innovate? What if generating more solutions evokes our hatred of creativity rather than our love of it? This chapter provides research data to address these questions and presents solutions for how we can generate ideas without sacrificing our ability to make them count.

In sum, the first half of this book chronicles why we resist creative change, and the second half chronicles how we can get ourselves and others to embrace it.

Creative
Change

1

The Hidden Innovation Barrier

WITHIN THE FIRST FEW MONTHS AFTER START-
ing my new position as an assistant professor at Wharton, I met
with a group of vice presidents who worked for a large global
company. For the sake of confidentiality, I'll refer to that business
as Company Z.

The VPs had determined that their company was struggling
with how to be more creative, and they asked me to present my
perspective on why this might be the case. I was extremely excited
about this meeting, in no small part because I knew the literature
cold — backward and forward. So like any good academic, I presented a summary of the research about how hard it is to generate creative (novel and useful) ideas and then actually implement
them.

I will never forget the look on the executives' faces after I finished my talk. I expected nodding heads, grunts of approval, or at
least some expressions of curiosity.

What I saw instead in their eyes was confusion and disappointment. Finally, one executive looked at me with skepticism and
said, "Yeah, but that isn't it."

Another executive was more patient with me. He explained
in detail the problem Company Z was having with creativity, and
it honestly had little to do with the material I had presented to

the group. "I wouldn't say that we struggle with generating creative ideas, or that implementation is the problem," the executive explained. "We can buy our creativity. We buy companies with breakthrough products, but these products rarely get to the implementation phase — and not because we don't know how to efficiently bring a product to market. Our problem is that once we buy these companies and integrate them under our umbrella, over time, they aren't creative anymore. Their pipeline dwindles and so we sell them off. But suddenly, only a short time later, those same companies that were vanilla are now developing creative products again."

He concluded: "If you want to help us figure out how to be more creative, figure out how to solve this puzzle, because, as far as we are concerned, that is the billion-, no, *trillion*-dollar question."

After this comment, I was rendered speechless (which, I can tell you, is a rare situation for me). The executives didn't agree with my traditional academic account of why creativity was so uncommon — it just didn't mesh with what they were experiencing. But if generating creative ideas wasn't the bottleneck, and implementation concerns weren't relevant to their situation, what then was the problem? This company didn't appear to be resistant to change — they were investing billions of dollars in creative products. So why were they struggling?

I soon learned that Company Z was not unique. Other companies — large, small, and in between — were struggling to be creative as well. Executives called and asked me to provide their organizations with training on creative-idea generation. Senior managers would tell me that creativity was a strategic priority for the company, but that their employees just weren't coming up with creative solutions.

Time after time, I conducted these trainings only to discover that most of the participants had already received training on idea generation. I would hear story after story of how employees had developed terrific ideas — which management promptly ignored. One participant even showed me a large stack of white papers she had written to document her many ideas — now in the file drawer. When I asked her why the company rejected her ideas when corporate leaders told me they were desperate for more creativity, she told me something I found quite surprising. She said, "Executives here don't actually want creative ideas."

That didn't make sense to me. Why would top-level executives at the very companies that were hiring me to help them be more creative spend a ton of resources to cultivate internal creativity, only to reject their employees' creative ideas? At best, it seemed like a blatant waste of money and other resources. At worst, it seemed like the essence of hypocrisy. Maybe all this talk about creativity was just lip service? I thought back to my meeting with Company Z — there's no way those busy executives would waste their time listening to consultants and spending billions of dollars on new companies if they were just pretending to want creativity.

Would they?

One thing was certain — executives wanted real solutions, and academics like me had spent decades identifying solutions. A quick search on the ABI Informs database (a database of business articles) shows that roughly 30,000 articles on creative idea generation — and 150,000 articles on implementation — have been published since the 1990s. Why, if we have all these solutions for how to generate and implement creative ideas, were companies still having a difficult time being creative?

If our best solutions weren't solving the problem, then maybe we needed to redefine the problem we were trying to solve. Was there an invisible third barrier to innovation beyond idea generation and implementation? If so, it must be so big that it could harm innovation, even in companies that were great at generating ideas and incredibly efficient at implementing them. Not only that, but it would have to be invisible to the decision makers whose job it was to innovate new solutions and convert opportunities into wins. So what was this invisible barrier?

As I pondered this question, I again considered the case of Company Z. Executives there told me that generating and implementing ideas was not the bottleneck they faced — they were certain of that. Instead, they believed that the companies they acquired became less creative over time. If this was indeed the case, then one possibility was that Company Z bought companies and then squelched their ability to generate creative ideas, perhaps due to loads of bureaucracy and paperwork. The problem with this logic was that Company Z was buying small companies that made medical devices, products that typically develop very slowly. From the time these companies were acquired to the time they were sold off, their products probably didn't change much at all.

I was on my own. I didn't have any answers, but I had a problem I was passionate about solving. I wanted to isolate this hidden barrier to innovation. And I had a hunch: maybe the executives at Company Z perceived the companies they had acquired differently over time *not* because the products had changed, but because *the way executives evaluated the products* had changed.

Were all of us operating using a false assumption? That is, we assume that any expert in a specific industry can accurately assess creative opportunity. We know that experts do a terrific job of evaluating products or processes that are familiar to them.

But what if creative ideas are so different from familiar and proven ideas that experts have a difficult time assessing them?

What if our fundamental assumptions about how we recognize and embrace creative opportunity are all wrong?

REVEALING OUR PARADOXICAL FEELINGS
ABOUT CREATIVITY

How could familiar ideas and new ideas be different? To under-stand, consider the following problem. Imagine that you are in a room with two large urns (see Figure 1). The urns are opaque, so you can't see inside them. But you know the urn on the left con-tains fifty white marbles and fifty black marbles. The urn on the right also contains one hundred marbles, but the ratio of white to black marbles is unknown.

> Here's the game: If you can draw a black marble in one pick,
> without looking, you win $100.
> Which urn do you draw from?

Figure 1. Two Urns.

One CEO told me that most of the decision-making team in his innovation group chose the urn on the left. In fact, when Dan-iel Ellsberg, formerly at the RAND Corporation, described this problem, he also found that most people chose the urn on the left. Chances are, you did too. Why?

Most people say that they chose the left urn because they felt this choice was a less-risky bet. But was it? The ratio of black to white marbles in the urn on the right was unknown, which means every ratio is as likely as any other. So the urn on the right could also have contained all black marbles, making your bet a sure thing. If you were to calculate the actual probability of drawing a black marble from the urn on the right, you might realize something surprising: the chance of picking a black marble from the urn on the right is 50 percent — exactly the same as picking a black marble from the urn on the left.

So if you chose the urn on the left simply because you thought it was a less-risky bet, then you didn't make your choice based on a rational problem-solving approach. Why then did you make this decision? Probably because you wanted to make your choice quickly, but also wanted to avoid uncertainty or a feeling of not knowing. Daniel Ellsberg identified an interesting paradox: even though both urns have the same probable payout, he found that people preferred the urn on the left because it allowed them to avoid ambiguity.

Amos Tversky, a professor of cognitive psychology at Stanford University, and Craig Fox, a professor of psychology at UCLA, found a fix to the Ellsberg paradox. If you evaluate each urn in the Ellsberg paradox problem separately, this ambiguity aversion goes away. It's only when you compare the two urns that you will become aware of ambiguity and so reject the uncertain option in favor of the seemingly more certain one. In other words, our aversion to ambiguity is not a given. Instead, it can come and go based on how we structure a problem.

In many ways, familiar ideas are like the urn on the left. We know a lot about them and how they operate, so we can calculate the risk of their functioning in the way we expect. But creative ideas are more like the urn on the right — we don't know a lot about them. That, however, is where the analogy ends. If you remember back to beginning algebra, you may recall a simple premise: If you have one known unknown in an equation, you can solve for X. If, however, you have two or more unknowns in a single equation, then calculating for X is impossible. And creative ideas tend to have many unknowns. We don't know exactly how creative ideas may benefit us in the future, or whether others will view us positively if we endorse them.

In the Ellsberg paradox, the uncertainty was knowable — you just had to take the time to do the mental math. Even this small amount of uncertainty feels pretty unsafe when compared to an easily knowable option. Now think how it might feel to encounter the kind of uncertainty you deal with when evaluating a creative idea where you can't know what you don't know.

Former U.S. secretary of defense Donald Rumsfeld famously said, "There are known knowns; there are things we know we know. We also know there are known unknowns; that is to say we know there are some things we do not know. But there are also unknown unknowns — the ones we don't know we don't know." You can calculate risk only when you have one known unknown. Creative ideas often involve many unknown unknowns. Interestingly, many innovation gurus will tell executives to calculate the risks or cost benefits associated with creative ideas. This made me wonder how people feel when confronted with the task of measuring something that is completely unknowable.

People often try to reduce uncertainty and find answers in unknowable situations. Think of the decision to get married. When you are contemplating marriage, would you run an equation to assess the risk of divorce? Would you calculate a number to determine if this person was a good match? If you said yes to these questions, you might be a budding social psychologist. But even with the terrific headway made in the last several decades, this field still can't figure out how to accurately predict whether a couple will divorce. Part of the problem is that there are so many unknowns. You don't know whether you might encounter financial difficulties during the course of your marriage, or if tragedy might strike, or whether your partner might fall in love with somebody else and decide to end the marriage on his or her own.

When you or someone you know is deciding whether or not to get married, you might raise these very concerns. You might ask, "How do I know this person is the one?" And then you would have received the barrage of useless advice everyone gives about what matters and what doesn't, only to realize that no one really knows the answer.

But you might notice your evaluation of your potential marriage partner shifting depending upon the advice you are given. One friend might say definitively, "When you know, you know. If you're even asking the question, this person is not the one." After you hear this, you might worry and think, *Oh no, I'm making a mistake.* But then you might ask another friend, who says, "You can't know, and everyone gets cold feet. It's going to be fine." This might make you feel calmer. Yet another friend might say, "Another person who is this great might never come along again." After hearing this, you might have a more optimistic outlook about your partner overall, even though you are still uncertain.

The point is this: how we frame our uncertainty can change the way we evaluate many different aspects of our lives — some quite important to our long-term success and happiness. So, why isn't this also true of how we evaluate creativity? I believe that it is.

Let's return to the example of the executives at Company Z and their decisions to buy or sell companies. When the executives decided to buy, they could have framed their uncertainty around the decision as tolerable (e.g., "This company has great potential, and we can't yet know if it will be profitable"). When the executives decided to sell, they could have framed their uncertainty as intolerable (e.g., "If we don't know with at least some accuracy that this company will be profitable, that means it is a bad investment").

Could it be that our ability to embrace creative ideas is *not* a purely rational process of calculating the odds, but instead a psychological process of simply managing our feelings of uncertainty? After all, these pesky doubts and what-ifs could cloud our judgment when choosing to embrace a creative idea. But if we aren't careful, we can be seduced by an idea that could ultimately bankrupt us. Could the struggle that the experts go through in evaluating creative ideas constitute this hidden barrier to innovation? And, if so, how would this barrier play out in the actual process of innovating?

CREATIVE CHANGE — THE HIDDEN INNOVATION BARRIER

Rosabeth Moss Kanter, professor of business at Harvard Business School, describes innovation as a three-stage process that starts with idea generation, progresses to decision making, and culminates in idea implementation. In her view, this model describes how innovation happens in large, formal organizations where employees come up with ideas and managers then decide which ones to pursue toward implementation.

But if you were to make her model more general, informal, and more specific to creativity, as opposed to decisions to implement familiar ideas, you might say that the decision-making stage can happen at many points in the innovation process. It can happen when you decide to use a specific creative idea of your own, or to convince others to use the idea. Both of these kinds of decisions could take place before any formal decision maker ever sets eyes on the idea.

Consider the opening sequence in the classic sci-fi film *2001: A Space Odyssey*. A group of prehistoric, apelike hominids are shown hanging around with lower animals by a small watering hole in an otherwise barren desert landscape. They drink and eat and groom one another peacefully — until a rival group wants to drink at the pool. Members of the rival clan scream and jump around, threatening to attack. And so the original group slowly backs away.

The pattern continues, until one day — after the sudden arrival of a strange black monolith in the original clan's camp — one of the "cavemen" stares at a large bone for a long time. He looks at his own hand, and then back at the bone. He then picks up the bone and swings it around, smashing other bones to pieces. The next frame shows the caveman bashing the head of one of the docile ungulates they live in association with, and the members of the clan eating its meat. The next time the rival clan arrives to frighten away the original group from the watering hole, the caveman uses a large bone to smash the enemy. Other members of his clan quickly join the fray, also using bones as weapons to win back the pond.

This example shows how creativity, albeit violent, wins the day; or perhaps it shows why we *believe* creativity wins the day. We assume that generating the creative idea to use the bone as a weapon gave the clan a competitive advantage over its rivals. Not only that, using the bone in battle actually worked. The original clan was able to launch a coordinated attack using bones as weapons. So we believe that winning with creativity requires that we both generate ideas and then figure out a way to effectively implement them.

But there is one more step that had to occur in order for the caveman's idea to win — a step that the film assumes is a given, a step you might assume is a given too. Put yourself, for a moment, in the caveman's shoes — or, more accurately, his feet. Imagine that you had the original insight that the bone could be used to smash things. Would you automatically decide to use the bone in a battle? Think about it. In battle, you are fighting an adversary who fights back, not a docile animal that doesn't see what is coming. You don't know for certain if using the bone against another of your kind will work and win the battle. The downside of using a bone and losing might pose a larger risk than simply running away as usual. After all, running away has suited your clan fine up to now. Your clan has managed to survive a long time, so why do you need to change your tactics? In contrast, using the bone might anger the other clan to such a degree that it might trigger a war that exterminates your people.

For that matter, in the movie, other members of the clan join the caveman, also using bones as weapons to fight the rival group. Imagine trying to convince your fellows to do something they had never conceived of before. Maybe they think you're a little odd and your ideas are strange or dangerous; they might not take you seriously. You might have to demonstrate how easy it is to smash things with the bone to win them over.

Even after demonstrating the value of the bone, some clan members might not be convinced and might tell others to ignore and ostracize you. One member might even laugh at you and tell others your idea is stupid. The reason is because, secretly, this clan member worries that this new use for bones will disrupt his high-status position as the only caveman strong enough to kill prey with his bare hands. The clan shaman might decide that using the bone will anger the ancestors, so he forbids its use, to avoid a disaster. In fact, you may even imagine a scenario where the rival clan has the same idea about using bones as weapons but decides, for all the reasons above, to reject it.

Obviously, once the clan uses the bone in battle and it defeats the enemy, there is a strong case to use the bone again in future. The bone no longer involves as many unknown unknowns once its value is proven, so you might use this fact to overcome any objections against using it.

My point is that, when that caveman first had the creative insight that the bone could serve as another kind of powerful fist, nobody had ever used a bone in battle before. The caveman couldn't guarantee success. The caveman couldn't say, "Listen, the other clan is using bones, so we should too." So, at this point, the psychology around how the caveman had to convince himself and others to use the bone was qualitatively different than the psychology around how to convince others to use the bone once it became a proven commodity.

This decision to embrace a creative idea is what I call *creative change*. The process of creative change involves *embracing a useful redefinition*. It means that for any person to undergo a creative change, he must move away from one way of defining something (e.g., a fist can be a weapon, but a bone cannot) to embrace a completely new and different way of defining this same thing (e.g., a bone is another kind of fist).

Creative change is part of the innovation process that is interwoven throughout the idea-generation and implementation stages. Creative change in organizations happens at many different levels. Creative change happens, for example, when you decide to use a creative idea — regardless of whether the idea is yours or someone else's. Creative change happens when venture capitalists green-light an innovative firm, or when organizational decision makers fund a new proposal. Creative change happens when critics laud the merits of the idea, and when consumers buy it. Creative change happens for others when you convince them to embrace a creative idea. For the caveman in *2001,* the creative change started when he decided to use the bone as a weapon in battle. Creative change continued when he convinced other cavemen, including the clan leader, to use it too.

Most people believe that the process of deciding to use a creative idea is simple — you want a creative idea, so you choose one. You might agree and insist that creative change is a no-brainer: the bone has an obvious use, so the caveman uses it. But that kind of thinking is hindsight, and it is colored by the total certainty you feel now that you know the idea worked. Instead, put yourself in the place of someone actually tasked with making that kind of decision *before* the end result is known. The caveman hopes the bone is useful and won't cause an all-out war his clan cannot win. But there is no guarantee that this will be the case. To see the bone as helpful enough to actually use in battle, the caveman had to manage his and others' uncertainty to overcome the what-ifs, and all the other concerns.

And people hold bias in favor of the status quo. The longer something has existed, the better we think it is. On average, the caveman and his clan were more likely to keep running away — and finding better and quicker ways to — than they were to adopt the new idea of using a bone as weapon.

In other words, recognizing a creative idea is not only about noticing that something is new. It is also about managing the inevitable uncertainty about whether the new thing actually solves the problem you have. With any creative idea there are layers of uncertainty to address and to resolve. First, you have to actually understand *why* the idea is more useful than the status quo. Then you need to manage your uncertainty about whether new ideas work reliably in different situations. And, of course, you need to manage the uncertainty that others will feel when they experience the new concept, too. Decades of research shows that people dislike and want to avoid uncertainty.

So if creative ideas are uncertain, and we dislike uncertainty, we also want to avoid creative ideas when they make us feel uncertain. I believe this is the essence of why it is so difficult to make creative change, and why creative change is the hidden barrier in the innovation chain.

CREATIVE CHANGES MAY BE INCONCEIVABLE, BUT THEY HAPPEN EVERY DAY

You might think that creative change happens so rarely, it is hardly worth spending time thinking about it. You are certainly familiar with high-profile creative changes, like our nearly universal adoption of the iPad and Uber — and those kinds of products and services aren't made available all that often.

In their forthcoming book *The Craft of Creativity,* professors Matt Cronin of George Mason University and Jeff Loewenstein of the University of Illinois at Urbana-Champaign describe that creative ideas often seem "inconceivable" — precisely because they require that we reinterpret our most basic assumptions and definitions to generate them.

Even though creative changes might seem rare and inconceivable, they can and do happen every day and in every aspect of our lives. This is because creative change is not restricted to our adoption of unusual products or physical objects. Creative change can happen when we change our definitions of a process, a specific group of people, someone we know, ourselves, or anything we can define.

Take the case of a very successful dermatology clinic that was thinking about expanding its offices. I had a chance to speak with the physician who was the managing partner in the clinic. He knew my field of study, so when we began speaking, he laughed. He said, "I'm not sure I'm very creative. I'm still trying to get my head around going from paper to electronic files." I raised an eyebrow and asked, "Don't most of your competitors use electronic files?" He laughed and said, "You know, for me, going electronic changes interactions with the patient. My clinic would be going from a reminder phone call from a nurse to a reminder text message generated by a computer. Now, when I meet with a patient, I browse through my manila patient folder while we talk. But, if our files were electronic, then I would sit at a desk, staring at a computer while talking to the patient. For me, this kind of change is really pushing me to reinterpret how I run my business. Yes, lots of clinics have already gone electronic. That doesn't mean it is an easy thing for my clinic to do."

The dermatologist described something I think many business-people feel. When people recognize a creative idea, they have to link their current definitions to new definitions that may seem impossible or even the opposite of the old way of doing things. This means that even if everyone else sees an idea as mundane, that idea could mean that, for you, a truly creative change is required.

We can also undergo creative change about how we view ourselves. I recently coached a CEO of a mid-sized sporting goods company. He had a big problem: no one in his company could agree on anything of importance to the organization. There was lots of conflict, and it was making the business and its people increasingly ineffective. Because the CEO defined himself as someone who wanted everyone to buy in, he decided not to take a side. The company ran into a stalemate, was stuck, and everyone was unhappy.

This CEO defined good leadership as helping his employees come to total agreement, and bad leadership as making decisions that employees didn't agree with. I pointed out that this definition was holding him back. I told him that he was operating like a politician, and asked if this was his intention.

The CEO did not like my calling him a politician, and he vehemently disagreed with me, because he believed politicians were uncaring, while his whole goal was to show real and sincere care for his employees. His attitude changed, however, when he received the exact same feedback from his subordinates. Once he acknowledged his definition as the problem, I worked with him to solve it. We redefined his role — transitioning from "politician" to "father figure" — an analogy that the CEO felt better reflected the role he wanted to play. Fathers can still care for their children and make decisions for them — even when children disagree. This analogy helped the CEO self-disrupt, get out of his own way, and start making the hard calls in the face of conflict.

This change in the CEO's approach was indeed creative change, the kind of change that can happen all the time, every day, in many aspects of our work and personal lives. Because creative change is a psychological process and not a rational one with an objective outcome, whether or not you undergo creative change isn't dependent upon how others think. Instead, creative change is dependent upon how *you* think. Creative change happens when you shift operations from an old definition to a new one.

Sometimes you don't need to undergo creative change to improve your company or your life. Returning to the caveman example, once your clan has embraced the use of the bone, you can change by improving your technique. You can use larger bones, or bones with sharper edges, or harder bones that will not break. This kind of improvement is important to keeping up with the competition. The problem is that it does not necessarily provide you with a clear advantage over your competition. Creative changes need to be new to an industry if they are going to provide you with a competitive advantage. For the caveman in *2001,* there was competitive advantage in adopting a bone as a weapon only because the rival clan had not yet done so. As soon as the rival clan adopts the concept, then swinging a femur becomes merely a standard or a necessity rather than a competitive advantage.

What I'm arguing here is that all creative changes involve some kind of innovation, but not all innovations involve creative change. The *Wall Street Journal* published an article in 2012 titled "You Call That Innovation?" describing the word *innovation* as jargon, a cliché. *Innovation* is one of those buzzwords that is so common it is starting to lose its meaning. Clayton Christensen at Harvard Business School describes the reason why quite nicely. He says that most of the "innovation" that companies engage in is really just another way to label continuous improvement so that they can keep up with the competitors.

In other words, innovation can happen without disrupting your current way of thinking. You can be innovative by improving the speed, or reducing the cost, or increasing the bandwidth of a product. Being innovative can include operating within an existing definition (e.g., implementing a mechanized process to make improvements). For example, if your definition of a mousetrap involves a device with springs and cheese, improving the trap by making the springs stiffer or the cheese more enticing would not require you to disrupt your thinking.

Making a creative change — even if that change seems mundane to everyone else — will always require that you disrupt your thinking before your behavior can follow suit. In contrast, you can make a change in behavior that does not require you to change the way you think (e.g., choosing to implement a more streamlined and efficient accounting program). When changes require creativity — moving from one definition to another — the psychological processes involved look totally different than when changes do not require creativity. Creative change is even more difficult and complicated to achieve than mere change. That said, even though creative changes are difficult, they happen all the time. So, if you let them, they can happen often for you too.

OUR BIAS AGAINST CREATIVE CHANGE

Why is creative change the hidden barrier to innovation? It is hidden because we love creative ideas. It is hidden because we have assumed that assessing a creative idea is a rational process with a knowable answer. It is hidden because we have assumed that when we desire creative ideas, all we need to do is choose some. It is hidden because scholars and practitioners have been focusing on solving the problem of creative-idea generation and its inherent implementation problems.

But if you start to think of creative change as a psychological process requiring us to manage the uncertainty that comes when we disrupt our current thinking, then a new picture emerges. Maybe we love creativity, but we also hate it.

To see this kind of emotional dynamic play out, read pretty much any article on artificial intelligence (AI). Scholars warn that beings with AI would have such superior intelligence to humans that they might view us with about as much care as we might view an ant, and so exterminate us without much thought. Scholars also note that AI can help us solve many pressing problems. AI can make us smarter, help us live longer — perhaps forever — and provide us with solutions to solve unexpected problems, such as an asteroid set to collide with Earth, or an extreme solar flare. If you watch any sci-fi at all, then you know the storyline where AI causes the apocalypse (e.g., *The Terminator, The Matrix, Battlestar Galactica,* etc.) as well as the one where AI fights to save the human race (e.g., *Interstellar,* the *Terminator* sequels, etc.).

Amidst all the intellectual banter and logical deductions is the fact that we are simultaneously enraptured and terrified by creative ideas. The discussion going on underneath all the speculation is simple: Uncertainty is something we either want to tolerate, or we don't.

The problem is that we have been attending to all the rational arguments about creative ideas without really considering how our feelings of uncertainty are coloring our "rational" assessments. Imagine making a decision about whether or not to fund a new idea right after managing a colossal innovation failure. Or imagine making the same decision after being hailed as an innovation champion. Both situations might influence this very important decision in overly negative or overly positive ways. If you don't take these strong feelings into account, then your decisions in the moment are not likely to be good ones.

Worse, what if we approach making creative changes as if they were rational and knowable? What kind of risk assessment would you use for something that is fundamentally unknowable? One executive told me that he basically just guessed. He said, "The way we assess risk for creative ideas is kind of like spinning a roulette wheel." Another decision maker told me that assessing risk for creative ideas was easy. Creative ideas have a really high failure rate, so all he did was place the creative idea in the extremely risky bucket. He also told me that if ideas are in that high-risk bucket, they are more likely to be rejected before the final decision makers ever get to see them.

Because companies often pursue a portfolio of ideas with a range of risk, they invest in only a relatively small handful of high-risk ideas. By the time decision makers actually sit down to decide which ideas to pursue, many high-risk ideas have already been weeded out by lower-level decision makers. The reason is that no lower-level decision maker wants to be pegged as the Pollyanna who keeps suggesting high-risk ideas to management.

If people have difficulty managing their uncertainty around whether new ideas will be useful, can they just consciously decide to adopt more creativity in their companies, and in their lives? Company Z couldn't. Even though executives at Company Z loved creativity and had tons of resources to invest in it, creativity still slipped through their fingers.

Many companies say they want innovation with creativity but they fail to achieve it. For example, in the early 2000s, 3M made the top ten on just about every "most innovative company" list that existed. It had generated many terrific products, such as the Post-it note and Scotch tape. It also implemented strong total quality management processes in the mid-2000s to improve their implementation tactics. Today, 3M continues to define itself as an innovative company, but its name no longer appears on any of the lists that once lauded its innovation prowess. In other words, 3M has shown competency in generating ideas; it has improved its ability to implement ideas without error. But neither of these activities is enough to push 3M back into the innovation spotlight. If employees, leaders, and managers within 3M lack an understanding of how to make creative change, great ideas that are also new won't have a chance to make impact even if 3M employees can generate and efficiently implement them.

In other words, winning with creativity does require someone to generate a creative idea, and it does require effective implementation. But merely having an idea won't help you much if you don't make the commitment to use it. Efficiently implementing a specific idea might not help you much either if your rival has a superior technology or if there is already a product that customers want more than the one you offer. For companies to reap real competitive advantage from ideas, a firm decision must be made to put creative ideas to use.

We have assumed that recognizing a creative idea is straightforward — if you want creativity, just choose to implement creative solutions. Of course, this approach doesn't work. It didn't work for Company Z. It didn't work for 3M. So what alternative do we have?

I believe creative change is a learned skill rather than a random process that is beyond a person's control to manage. Just as you can have expertise in a given domain, like chemical engineering, for example, you can also have expertise in leading the process of creative change. If you are a leader, learning how to embrace creativity can help you identify the corporate vision to move your company in productive new directions, rather than unwittingly embracing a vision that will take your company down a path of uncreative destruction. If you are a leader, then embracing a creative corporate vision is not enough, because your employees could have a bias against creative change. Leaders must learn how to get subordinates to buy into their creative visions. Further, it is not enough for leaders to merely encourage creativity in subordinates. Leaders also need to build systems that can recognize, utilize, and commit to the creative solutions produced. Managing creative change is a key leadership skill. Instead of reacting to creative solutions when they come and rejecting them (or watching helplessly as others reject your creative ideas), you can proactively manage the process of making creativity count.

CONCLUSION

We have assumed that creative ideas can be evaluated using the same metrics and procedures that we employ to evaluate familiar ideas. For familiar ideas, you can assess risk and compare risk assessments in a portfolio of ideas and choose the best one (least risk, highest returns). But what is the risk of a creative idea succeeding? The truth is, according to Dean Simonton, an eminent social psychologist, unless you are a prophet or psychic, you can't know.

Creative change is thus the hidden barrier in the innovation chain because we falsely believe that we love creative ideas, that we are truly open to and accepting of them. There are entire industries built on lauding the merits of creativity. But the hard reality is that when we try to assess the future value of creative ideas using real numbers, these assessments tend to be overly negative. And that's a real problem.

But there is a silver lining. Now that we know that the decision to adopt a creative idea is more of a psychological process than a rational one, we can gain some control back around how to make these kinds of decisions. We can learn to make creative change. But to do so, we need to deeply understand ourselves and the psychology that has been holding us back and keeping us from adopting the very solutions that make our lives and our companies better.

2

Our Love-Hate Relationship
with Creativity

DO PEOPLE HATE CREATIVE IDEAS?

Ask most anyone, and the answer would be a resounding *No!*
Business executives will tell you that creative ideas drive the development of new products and services, and they lead to cost-saving techniques that enhance the bottom lines of their companies.
Scholars will tell you that creativity fuels human progress, corporate competitive advantage, and scientific discovery. Artists, musicians, and other creatives will tell you that they live and breathe creativity — it's their reason for being.

Indeed, if you Google "creative," you get well over 1.6 billion webpages. That is almost ten times more hits than you get Googling "how to get rich," and four times more hits than Googling "happiness"!

Businesses today spend millions of dollars on creativity consultants, workshops, and related activities. Of the twenty most popular TED talk videos of all time, the *most* popular of all is about creativity. IBM recently asked 1,500 executives which leadership characteristics were most desired, and number one was, you guessed it, creativity. The topic of creativity in business has become so commonplace today that the *Huffington Post* recently referred to creativity business books on the *New York Times* bestseller list as clichéd, and *The Atlantic* published an article claiming that "Americans worship creativity."

My colleagues Jeffrey Loewenstein, Jennifer Deal (at the Center for Creative Leadership), and I ran a study that examined which product features customers wanted. We asked *decision makers* in a company to rate thirty-two new products to get their sense as to whether they were profitable, feasible, or creative. We then asked *customers* to rate these same thirty-two products in terms of how eager they were to buy each one. Not surprisingly, we found that *product creativity* — not *perceived profitability* — was the strongest predictor of customers' desire to buy products.

All this love for creativity is just what we would expect — we all want more creativity and more new ideas in our organizations, right?

Not necessarily. In fact, there is a growing body of evidence that indicates something quite the opposite.

Research has found that resistance to new ideas occurs in every domain: the workplace, school, academia, sciences, government, and our personal lives. And because creative ideas have the potential to improve our lives in so many ways, we pay a steep price when we ignore them in favor of less optimal, more traditional solutions. For example, digital photography technology was invented by Kodak engineer Steve Sasson, but his creative idea was placed in the file drawer by Kodak management long before digital photography became the industry standard — and long before Kodak's *uncreative destruction,* when it declared bankruptcy because the company had been so reticent to embrace the digital age.

In the study above, where we had decision makers rate thirty-two new products on how feasible, creative, and profitable each one was, we also correlated these ratings with whether the decision makers actually implemented these product ideas. We found that decision makers decided to implement only the most familiar and feasible product ideas — *the ideas with the lowest levels of creativity* — even though those ideas were liked least by customers and seen as low in profitability by C-suite executives and, ironically, by the decision makers themselves.

This suggests that experts and people in important and key roles are not always making good decisions when it comes to choosing creative ideas. But why aren't they? Is this something specific just to decision makers, or is there a broader problem — one that is potentially even more troubling?

The question of why we desire but resist creative ideas is difficult to study, because if you ask people in a straightforward way about creativity, chances are you won't get a straightforward answer. Early in my academic career, I interviewed a host of people (e.g., doctors, lawyers, executives), asking them what role creativity played in their everyday work. Surprisingly, the results were more puzzling than enlightening. One manager in a pharmaceutical company said: "Creative? I'm not an artist! If I do something totally wacky I could kill a patient, and the firm could have a huge lawsuit on its hands." To which I responded, "So being creative is really not part of your everyday work?" The manager snapped back, "I take offense to that. I *have to be* innovative. If I'm not pushing the boundaries of what we know, then people could die."

When I asked what role creativity played for a decision maker at a Fortune 500 company with a corporate strategy around innovation as a means of competing in the marketplace, the executive said, "What we want are ideas that are innovative in that they appeal to a broad range of customers, are feasible to produce, and fit with our brand strategy." When I again asked, "So, what about creativity?" the executive responded by saying: "Creativity? I don't care about whether products are creative! I care about whether the products make a profit!"

The most striking example of how people think about creativity came from an executive at Apple who said the following: "Let me channel Steve Jobs for a minute. Why do I care if ideas are creative? I only care whether ideas are great!"

What these responses revealed to me was that people at work won't tell you outright that they dislike creativity. Instead, they are more indirect and discreet in their criticism of creative ideas. They will tell you that creativity is too mushy and difficult to measure, and as such, too wishy-washy to bet on; or they'll say that creativity is a fine thing, but irrelevant to meeting their goals. If you look deeply into the academic literature about best practices in everyday decision making, you will quickly see that the scholars who wrote these articles don't talk about creativity either. Instead, they recommend that when you are making any decision, the *quality* of the idea is the most important thing to consider (e.g., whether the idea is feasible, risky, profitable, etc.), and they ignore creativity. The same is true for the innovation literature. That's right, you will be hard pressed to find a book on innovation that clearly links creativity to how people choose the new ideas they want to implement.

Take innovation guru Clayton Christensen. One of his big ideas was that disruptive technologies can upset market hierarchies — so you can be on the top of the market one minute, but abruptly thrown into the middle or the back of the pack when some other company brings a new technology to market that makes yours less relevant (as online streaming of movies made the DVD rental market virtually disappear). Christensen often identified low cost as a key feature of disruptiveness, which explains why he predicted that the iPhone would not be disruptive. After all, the first iPhone had a high price point and delivered high quality — two components that did not match up with his view of which technologies would dominate in the marketplace. And yet, as we well know, iPhones went on to totally disrupt and dominate the market for portable electronics for years.

To this day, I have never understood why Christensen did not include creativity in the list of features that can identify a technology as disruptive. This was especially striking to me when Jeffrey Loewenstein and I ran a study asking hundreds of participants in the United States to nominate creative products. We found that the most commonly nominated product was — drum roll, please — the iPhone.

So while people may worship creativity, they also seem to distrust and discredit creative ideas and thus ignore creativity as an important consideration — even if creativity is clearly relevant to the problem being solved. What makes this even more complicated to disentangle is that people do not like to openly admit that they hate creativity.

After my research team Shimul Melwani (of University of North Carolina at Chapel Hill), Jack Goncalo (at Cornell University), and I published our paper "Bias against Creativity," I received many emails from people who had read the article and felt as though the paper explained and validated why their own creative ideas had been dismissed by the powers that be. But here is the thing: It is not merely the powerful doctor, professor, decision maker, or boss who rejects and dislikes creativity. The person who rejects and dislikes creativity is *you*.

This truth may shock you since, after all, you are taking the time to read this book, so you must care about creative change and want to foster it. Yet, my work reveals that even though we say that we love and desire creativity, we can and will still reject creative ideas under certain circumstances. That is, me, you, the late Steve Jobs, everyone, even those who are the most open to new ideas, can reject creative ideas in certain situations.

So what are those circumstances that make us — and the decision makers in our lives, at work, at home, and in our communities — so resistant to the solutions that would otherwise transform our lives in remarkably positive ways?

HOW MINDSETS SHAPE OUR ABILITY TO RECOGNIZE CREATIVE POTENTIAL

Robert, a star engineer, works for a company that actively encourages creativity by allowing all of its employees to use 10 percent of their hours to work on new ideas to help improve company processes. This is one of the reasons Robert took the job, because he enjoys solving new and difficult problems and he wanted to feel challenged at work. Sure enough, after developing a great idea that he was certain would have a significant positive impact for his employer, Robert then decided to pitch the idea internally to the decision-making team tasked with funding new ideas for development.

Robert wears a suit (so they will take him seriously) and comes armed with PowerPoint slides and a well-rehearsed, five-minute pitch. The pitch details a new engineering solution to a big problem the company has had for many years. The solution would require that the company use existing resources in a new way, which is appealing but has never been tried by anyone in the organization (though it has been used in other industries). Robert's final slide shows how the solution will require a $1 million investment by the company, but that it can save increasing amounts of money over time — a projected total of $50 million in the five years after implementation. The classic hockey stick.

The members of the decision-making team nod their heads slowly — almost in unison — and several purse their lips. "Interesting idea," one decision maker says. "But how do you know that you can fix the problem for one million dollars?"

Robert clears his throat and explains in detail how he came up with the figure.

The decision maker, though, isn't satisfied with this answer. He asks, "But based on what data did you arrive at your conclusion?"

Robert shows his discomfort and tells the truth: "No other company in our industry has done anything like this before. I gave it my best guess."

Another decision maker raises her eyebrows. "Do you have project management experience? I would imagine that kind of experience would help you accurately estimate this kind of expense."

Robert puffs out his chest and says, "Well, I won the Best Contributor award last year in the engineering department." To which the decision maker says, "So that would be a 'no,' then."

"Thank you, Robert," another decision maker says, almost impatiently. "We want and need new and fresh ideas to continue the company's growth trajectory, and we appreciate your taking the time. Unfortunately, we can't spend that kind of money based solely on some untested assumptions you generated."

Frustrated, Robert leaves and immediately sets up a meeting with his supervisor to talk about moving from an engineering to a management position. Robert's supervisor is open to this change, but she asks other managers for feedback about Robert's leadership potential before making a commitment. The general consensus is that Robert seems creative, but his asking for a million-dollar investment with no proof of concept gave the leadership team pause. Some say Robert is too naive and inexperienced for a leadership role. Others believe he is probably a good engineer, but good engineers don't often make good managers. They say that engineers tend to focus on expensive engineering solutions that they find interesting, not on more feasible but perhaps less interesting management solutions that are more likely to be cost-effective.

Robert's supervisor takes this feedback to heart and tells Robert to apply again for a management track in a couple of years, after he has had a bit more experience. Now incensed, Robert starts working on his résumé, thinking he would love to work for an established company — or even a startup — where creativity is truly encouraged. When Robert resigns from the company a few months later to go work at a competitor, his supervisor is disappointed, but not surprised.

In this scenario, Robert is in an impossible situation. He knows you can't have unimpeachable data that shows with absolute certainty that a new idea will work when that idea has never been tried before. Robert tries to influence decision makers by playing what he sees as "the game." He dresses the part, has PowerPoint slides, a reputation as a terrific engineer, and carefully constructed numbers that show substantial corporate gains from his proposed investment. He learned all these tactics and more from an idea-selling workshop he attended earlier in the year. But what he also comes to realize is that all this preparation just isn't enough. He missed a key ingredient in his recipe for success.

Before we get to that missing ingredient, we first need to understand the power that one's mindset has in whether or not new ideas are adopted.

A *mindset* is a set of beliefs or a way of thinking that can be activated (or not) by your disposition or environment. When it comes to creativity, two mindsets are of particular interest:

- **How/best** Focuses the evaluators on knowing the most feasible and appropriate option now. This mindset is intolerant of uncertainty.

- **Why/potential** Focuses the evaluators on learning the future value of something. This mindset is much more tolerant of uncertainty.

Absent any other factors, a pure how/best mindset can undervalue the future potential of a creative idea relative to a practical one. As a result, decision makers who are in a how/best mindset will instinctively tend to reject new ideas in favor of maintaining the status quo.

At Robert's presentation, the decision makers were clearly in a how/best mindset — that is what the literature on decision making, innovation, and everything they learned from their finance and accounting classes suggested they should do. For decision makers the how/best mindset is a best practice!

From a how/best perspective, the most important problem to solve is whether or not the idea in question is a good one. In this case, *good* is defined as immediately feasible and cost-effective. What is interesting about this problem-solving approach is that it completely ignores the actual problem Robert is attempting to solve. A how/best perspective isn't concerned with whether the idea in question could be modified or adjusted to solve the problem. Nor does a how/best perspective consider whether Robert could prove himself in the future by leading a committee to investigate additional solutions to the problem, or to make the current solution more cost-effective.

For a person in a how/best mindset, *solving* the problem is not the ultimate goal. Instead, the goal is *evaluating* the solution in question. But to evaluate something accurately right now, you need to make one big assumption; you must assume that the idea being evaluated won't change or improve. The idea is *static* — it is what it is. The problem with this approach, of course, is that when it comes to creative ideas, we know this assumption is false. Creative ideas are likely to change and to improve, whereas proven and familiar ideas tend to be more static. This is another reason why a how/best approach is a poor fit for the demands of evaluating a creative idea relative to a familiar one.

Of course, assuming that all ideas are static helps make the complexity and uncertainty around these kinds of decisions much more manageable. People in a how/best mindset have goals in making decisions efficiently. My research team and I have evidence that this may also mean that those in a how/best mindset are more likely to use stereotypes or lay beliefs when making decisions under uncertainty. While making decisions when faced with uncertainty, people in a how/best mindset will employ stereotypes because they allow them to quickly and efficiently categorize things and make decisions with relatively little cognitive effort.

For example, it might surprise you that Robert's hockey-stick graph didn't hold much sway with decision makers. You might take this to indicate that the decision makers are devoting some serious mental muscle to thinking through the problem. Actually, the decision makers in Robert's presentation were using a mental shortcut. Decision makers are quite familiar with the hockey-stick graph, which shows exponential profits or cost savings over time. The reason is that a hockey-stick graph is a best practice for selling ideas. So, to decision makers, a hockey-stick graph is something that is merely expected rather than something that distinguishes one idea from another. Instead of being blown away by the numbers, the decision makers questioned whether Robert's numbers were credible.

To get a sense of whether Robert's numbers made sense, the decision makers used another kind of shortcut. They examined Robert himself. It is very common for decision makers to look to specific qualities and characteristics of the inventor or idea champion to reduce uncertainty around whether an idea is a good bet. But notice which traits the decision makers in their how/best mindset are attending to. The decision makers don't pay much attention to Robert's technical expertise, or anything indicating whether his idea would actually work and fix the problem. The decision makers instead looked at traits Robert exhibited to discern whether his cost estimates were accurate and whether he could efficiently implement his solution.

When we want to make assessments quickly about things we do not know or understand, we often draw upon what we believe to fill in the gaps. We can also hold stereotypes, or shared beliefs, about the traits exhibited by a certain group of people. These stereotypes and beliefs spawn from when we talk to others, see examples in the media, and socialize with work colleagues. For example, I later asked one of the decision makers in that meeting why she asked whether Robert had management experience to vet his idea. She admitted to me that she had recently returned from a conference where many of the attendees (all senior managers in large organizations) had complained that their engineers constantly come up with expensive ideas that don't make any business sense. She mentioned having relayed this very story to other members of the decision-making team immediately before Robert's presentation.

So the bigger-picture view is this: A stereotype or lay belief about engineers not being business savvy was transmitted to the decision-making team through a process of socialization. In this case, the first step involved one decision-making team member interacting with a credible group that exposed the decision maker to the idea that engineers lack business savvy and experience. This decision maker then related this belief to other decision makers in her own group, and then used this very belief in the course of vetting Robert's presentation.

The fact that Robert, an engineer, admitted he didn't have any management experience served to confirm for these decision makers that the stereotype was real, powerful, and important. For this reason, the group is likely to continue to use this stereotype to make funding decisions in the future.

My point is not that stereotypes are right or wrong in principle. Rather, I argue that these stereotypes help us efficiently manage situations that are laden with uncertainty and that people in how/best mindsets may be more likely to use and rely on stereotypes. In sum, Robert's idea never had a chance. Because Robert was an engineer with no management experience, pitching a new idea to this decision-making team was doomed from the start.

There is a second, simpler reason why Robert's approach wasn't going to be accepted. In the how/best mindset, uncertainty is a red flag. And, worse, the how/best mindset makes people pay closer attention to all the ways in which new ideas are uncertain. This hypervigilance means that people in the how/best mindset will immediately zero in on the greatest weakness of any creative idea — because no one has experience implementing it yet, the idea is not proven. Decision makers will see your very positive projections and ask a very reasonable question, "Where did you get this data?" And when you tell them that it's the best-case scenario, based strictly on assumptions, it's essentially telling the decision makers that your data is based on unknowns — something people in a how/best mindset will always avoid, never embrace.

Someone in a how/best mindset will tend not to see a new idea as a good and viable option relative to an existing solution because there is often more uncertainty around whether the new idea will result in the achievement of any specific goal. If that uncertainty is framed as something unresolvable (as happens when we wish to show accurate data about any untried creative idea), it can make a person feel anxious and fearful — two emotions we always prefer to avoid.

This is why, from the decision makers' vantage point, by rejecting Robert's idea they may have missed an opportunity to make the company millions of dollars, but they also saved themselves from the anxiety of having to justify to their bosses why they spent $1 million on a project that failed, when there was no "good or reliable" data to indicate future success.

THE POWERLESSNESS OF RATIONAL
PERSUASION WHEN PITCHING CREATIVE IDEAS

There is another aspect to Robert's story that is important to note. The influence strategies recommended in the power-and-influence literature can sometimes backfire when promoting creative ideas. For example, experts such as Robert Cialdini and Gary Yukl might suggest that someone should rely on her expertise and rational persuasion to sell a new idea. However, the following example illustrates why rational persuasion attempts can have unwanted results when pitching creative ideas to someone who has a how/best mindset.

Dr. Smith (the names in this true story have been changed for confidentiality) is a gastroenterologist — a physician specializing in the gastrointestinal tract. Gastroenterologists are trained to perform endoscopy or colonoscopy, procedures that survey the digestive tract and allow the physician to document any anomalies (e.g., polyps) and also remove them, if needed.

Dr. Smith also has an entrepreneurial spirit and so is always looking for new ways to improve patient care at her hospital. As a result, she decides to pitch a revolutionary new technology — the

PillCam, a camera in pill form, which the patient swallows, that takes photos of the patient's digestive system as it moves through it — to Dr. Glascoe, the physician who is her supervisor. Dr. Smith knows that Dr. Glascoe's top priorities are safety and quality patient care, so she makes sure to emphasize these angles when she pitches the PillCam.

Dr. Smith tells Dr. Glascoe that the PillCam requires approximately the same prep as colonoscopy or endoscopy, but it is much safer because it does not require anesthesia, as endoscopy and colonoscopy do, and it avoids the risk of damaging the patient's organs with the metal probes used in those procedures. Not only that, but PillCam eliminates the possibility of a physician performing an unplanned biopsy on the spot. (An unplanned biopsy during endoscopy led to Joan Rivers's death in 2014.) Dr. Smith also made sure to mention that patients reported that they like the PillCam more than traditional endoscopy and colonoscopy because they can watch their scan in real time and can also have a recorded video to use if they need a second opinion about treatment. Dr. Smith also noted that the PillCam won the *Wall Street Journal* Innovation Award, and that it has been safely used for more than a decade.

Dr. Glascoe listens to this pitch and asks reasonably, "If the PillCam is so safe and so much better than traditional means, why isn't it used more widely? Our rival hospitals aren't using it."

"Well," Dr. Smith starts, "many of the insurance companies decided either not to cover it or to offer only $200 reimbursement for the procedure."

"Why is that?" asks Dr. Glascoe, to which Dr. Smith shrugs her shoulders and shakes her head; she has no answer. Dr. Glascoe looks at her and says, "Insurance companies carefully examine all the data, so I'm sure that if this procedure was really safe and cost-effective, they would reimburse for it. But since they don't, I can't see offering it here. What patient would want to pay an additional $500–$1,000 for a procedure that won't be covered by their insurance?"

"A patient who is concerned about the relative health risks of endoscopy," responded Dr. Smith.

"That may be," Dr. Glascoe replied, "but we have limited resources as it is, and endoscopy and colonoscopy are still needed if the patient requires more than just a scan via PillCam, right? If we add the PillCam to the list of procedures we offer, we are adding yet another burden of having to learn something new on our physicians, who are already overloaded with responsibilities. No, I'm sorry, Dr. Smith, but I just don't see how this helps us improve patient care."

Dr. Smith was totally surprised at the outcome of this meeting. She did not expect Dr. Glascoe to reject the PillCam idea — it seemed to her like a slam dunk, a sure thing. Later that year, the hospital was sued for harming a patient during a routine endoscopy, and when Dr. Smith signed the paperwork indicting her (all physicians in a division are sued in these cases — even if they didn't work on the patient directly), she thought very seriously about quitting her job.

The PillCam is a demonstrably better scanning tool than endoscopy and colonoscopy. So here is a rare case where the new solution has sufficient data to prove with certainty that it is superior to the status quo. Because so much data about the solution exists, it would seem that straight-up rational persuasion would be the most effective means of influencing a decision maker like Dr. Glascoe.

Note how the how/best mindset works. Even this level of certainty about idea quality is not enough, because for someone with a how/best mindset, there are always other aspects of implementation to consider, and they might highlight the uncertainty of any new idea.

Anything new to an organization — even if it seems standard and mundane to the outside world — comes fraught with uncertainties to the people in charge of implementing it. I remember having a conversation with my local dry cleaner because he was nervous about switching from his paper-and-pencil bookkeeping system to Microsoft Office. My dry cleaner's worries were not unfounded. He encountered a slew of mistakes during the implementation process that he had simply not anticipated. One day, for example, his computer powered down automatically to install the latest Windows update, and he lost some data; it became clear that he needed to do more work to make the new software and hardware function the way he needed them to.

In other words, to someone with a how/best mindset, the fact that the idea or solution is clearly superior in an *objective* sense isn't always enough to warrant implementing it. Objective data about how superior one solution is to another is not always sufficient to make a decision maker feel safe about the implementation concerns.

So what *would* satisfy a how/best mindset? I cover several possible solutions elsewhere in this book, but I'll say for now that while it seems like Dr. Glascoe is being rational and methodical in his decision making, when you look at his objections more closely, they aren't necessarily rational. That is, Dr. Glascoe does not actually know why insurance companies rejected the PillCam, or why rival hospitals aren't using the PillCam. Nor does he know patients' actual interest and willingness to pay for a PillCam procedure over more traditional means, or if other physicians in his division will resist having to learn a new procedure.

In other words, he is rejecting this idea without gathering data to address all the known unknowns, and instead he simply assumes that because competitors are not using the PillCam, his belief that all the known unknowns likely point to the PillCam being suboptimal is supported. His assumption that if the product were so great others would be using it already is circular, and therefore irrational, because the entire reason why the product is not yet widely used is because it is still *new,* and new products are — by definition — less proven.

So could Dr. Smith have prepared her pitch more effectively by gathering all the data and better answering the known/unknowns? Maybe. But in my experience, the how/best mindset is also quite clever at thinking up all sorts of unknown unknowns — the kind of objections that the person pitching or implementing the idea can never plan for. That's the coup de grâce of the how/best mindset.

After all, what if the PillCam is discredited and harms patients in the future? What if another newer and better technology comes around and replaces the PillCam by the time these doctors have trained everyone in their division to use it? What if the manufacturer goes out of business? What if the cloud storage of PillCam data is hacked and patient privacy rights are violated? There is an unlimited number of potential unknown unknowns around Pill-Cam. And while there are some good counters to the what-if strategy of idea rejection, they are not necessarily grounded in great data to refute these fears.

What this also means is that a traditional selling approach of overcoming all objections with good data might not work when selling creative change to someone with a how/best mindset. When it comes to selling that idea, having great data can be neither necessary nor sufficient to convince a decision maker. And sometimes having great data can merely corner a person with a how/best mindset into the position of using their what-if method of idea rejection.

Again, it is important to note that Dr. Glascoe's how/best

mindset might be very effective for other decisions he needs to make. For example, if he performs an emergency procedure, he needs to efficiently and accurately use available solutions to solve a problem on the spot. A how/best mindset is well suited to the demands of a situation where a person may need to decide swiftly — and where existing solutions are adequate to solve the problem.

Is the how/best mindset actually more efficient at accurately vetting the PillCam idea? After all, to gather data on all the known unknowns (let alone on the possible unknown unknowns) is a daunting task — especially since Dr. Glascoe says that time and other resources are slim in his department. So in the short term, the how/best mindset would seem to be the right problem-solving approach to follow.

Of course, there are several critical flaws in this argument. First, the PillCam idea already has an internal champion, Dr. Smith, who has implicitly agreed to help gather more information about it on her own time. Dr. Glascoe is unfortunately so caught up in his short-term perspective that he cannot see this wonderful opportunity. In addition, since the hospital was subject to a significant lawsuit and the subsequent loss of millions of dollars, working to make the PillCam technology available would have seemed an obvious way to go. But now, because of the lawsuit, the hospital's cash reserves are diminished even further, making it even less likely that Dr. Glascoe would embrace a new solution like the Pill-Cam. When it comes to learning and embracing new information, the how/best mindset can really get in the way.

YOU MAY BE BIASED AGAINST CREATIVE IDEAS

We have seen that it's quite possible for people in a variety of circumstances to be biased against creative ideas. But now, what about *you*? Is it possible that you might harbor some of these same biases against creativity?

Consider the example of Jonathan, a student of engineering at a university. Jonathan needs to have a certain grade point average in order to qualify for good internships and to land a great job after graduation. He is creative and open to many possibilities, but when he walks into his ethics class, he is immediately uncomfortable. The instructor says there are no right answers but many possible ways to think about the same problem — not like in his accounting or chemistry classes, where there is only one best solution. The teacher begins ethics class with a discussion that is unfocused and goes in many different directions. As such, it is not clear to Jonathan what exactly will be covered on the final exam.

Later in the course, Jonathan asks for a specific outline of all the topics covered in class that will be on the exam. The professor provides him with one, but she adds that the exam will require students to think creatively, and so he will need to integrate topics and analyze problems — not just memorize information. Jonathan is uncomfortable and concerned about this approach, so he asks the professor what she means by "thinking creatively," if she can give him a clear example of how that will manifest on the exam, and a rubric of exactly how the exam question will be graded.

The professor tells Jonathan that creativity is defined as the ability to produce something that is new and potentially useful, and, as an example, she shares with him an answer from a prior exam that she thought was really creative. The professor emphasizes that the current exam will have a different question, of course, and that there is no grading rubric because every student's answer will likely be different. Jonathan is now extremely worried about this kind of exam and confused about how to prepare and study.

Sure enough, he studies everything on the exam outline, but

in the end, receives only an average grade. He then becomes angry and blames the professor. After all, if the professor were being fair, she would have provided a lot more formal structure to her students.

In contrast, Sam is another student in the same ethics class as Jonathan, but she approaches the class very differently. When Sam hears the professor saying there is no best solution, she feels intrigued and energized. She wonders why, and after lecture has many additional questions for the professor. When Sam comes to office hours, she discusses her ideas with her professor and asks whether there are additional readings she might do to help her prepare for the exam. Before the test, Sam answers a study question and then gives her answer to the professor for comments. The professor delightedly provides Sam with feedback. Sam receives an A in the class and feels like she learned something new in her approach to problem solving.

We can see that Jonathan approaches the class with a how/best mindset as he focuses intently on finding the most effective means of studying and receiving a good grade with minimal wasted effort. That is, Jonathan is concerned with *how* — specifically, *how* to study and *how* the exam will be graded. Jonathan frames the exam in terms of providing the *best* answers, and he defines *best* in terms of accuracy, because he assumes accuracy is what leads to a high grade. He is also concerned with efficiency. He wants a study guide so he can focus on only the material that is directly relevant to the exam so he will earn a high grade.

In contrast, Sam views the same situation from a why/potential mindset. Sam wants to know *why*, and she is excited by the universe of possibilities. Like Jonathan, Sam also feels uncertain that she might not know the answers, but her uncertainty manifests totally differently — as curiosity. Unlike Jonathan, Sam does not freak out and feel she doesn't know what to do. Instead of thinking about how she can go about studying, Sam is focused on finding out why she does not understand the problem completely. Like Jonathan, Sam also seeks to resolve her uncertainty, but instead of getting caught up in the details, she reads more widely and has discussions with her professor. For Jonathan, uncertainty is experienced as negative and destructive, whereas for Sam, uncertainty becomes a positive and facilitates her learning.

A how/best mindset is well suited to any situation in work, school, or life where there is a correct answer or where the means of finding the answers is formulaic and predictable (such as solving a math problem with an existing formula). The reason that how/best mindsets work in these contexts is because there exists a *predictable and reliable* way of solving problems efficiently and accurately.

Because how/best mindsets are often efficient at problem solving in a variety of situations, they can be overutilized and reinforced even in contexts where problems cannot or should not be solved in predictable or reliable ways. Institutions can perpetuate a cycle of how/best thinking. While we can't know who started the cycle in the university above, students in a how/best mindset crave structure because it allows them to obtain good grades more efficiently and with less uncertainty. In turn, they view the kind of rigid structure in which they can excel as indicating that a professor is "good." Hence, universities that place a high value on professors' course evaluation ratings for promotion and tenure decisions may unintentionally pressure professors to adopt a more structured how/best approach to teaching. Students then take more classes where professors adopt a how/best kind of approach — and learn to expect this approach and rate professors accordingly.

If mindsets can be activated by our environment, it points to an important silver lining. Decades of research show that we can easily manipulate whether a person is in a how/best or a why/potential mindset, mimicking in the lab what happens organically in our lives. Social psychologists call this *priming;* it involves giving subjects in an experimental setting a task to complete that activates a specific way of thinking for a short period of time. Priming is the reason why Jonathan could, in fact, be a highly creative student while also entrenched in a how/best mindset, because our situations in the world can prime us into either mindset.

But the bad news is that the how/best mindset can be especially paradoxical because people who are in it might reject creativity even if they believe they want it. I asked those who rejected creative ideas in the scenarios above (i.e., the decision makers in Robert's presentation, Dr. Glascoe, et al.) if they desired creative solutions. All said yes — they really wanted that. More specifically, one person said, "Our problem is that we just can't find creative ideas to fund. If we had more of them, we would fund them." Another person chimed in, "The engineers here are just not creative. I mean, if they were really creative, they would be working for themselves in a startup, making lots of money. The problem with corporate America is that we attract the most stable worker bees — sticks in the mud who just want stability. This makes it hard when you want to shake things up."

These responses meant to me that the people who rejected creative ideas in these cases were not aware or willing to acknowledge that they were exhibiting a bias against creative ideas. Each person thought he or she was acting in a solid, rational, and deliberative manner and making good decisions. So we're back to square one. Even *you* may be biased against creative ideas and not want to acknowledge or realize it. And if you have this tendency to reject creative ideas, you're probably unaware that you may be driving away opportunities to enrich your life with creative change. Worse, you may even blame others for the lack of creative solutions in your own life.

Let's face it, our lives are busy and we are always trying to figure out how to juggle tasks more efficiently. To make matters even more problematic, every social psychologist I know will tell you that the world has become more complicated. Information is more readily available, and we have more choices now than ever before. We need our stereotypes, beliefs, and tendencies toward pattern recognition more than ever, because these are the basic building blocks of cognitive economy and efficiency. We don't have time to deeply process and gather all the data to make every decision. But this also means that today — more than ever — we are likely to be chronically addicted to the how/best mindset, even when that mindset is maladaptive, because we need creative solutions, not traditional ones.

In my experience, how/best mindsets are often well suited to address situations that mainly involve concerns around efficiency (e.g., getting to work on time, studying for a multiple-choice test, using an existing process to implement a solution or product). A how/best mindset is a good match for situations where the best solution is knowable. However, there are times when the situation calls for creative exploration, and the how/best mindset is a poor match for those times. There are also situations where efficiency concerns compete with novelty concerns. In these contexts, the how/best mindset is especially tricky; it would *seem* to match the situation appropriately because efficiency does matter. But the situation *also* calls for novelty, and as a result, a pure how/best mindset is problematic because it inaccurately evaluates the novelty aspect of any idea in an overly negative manner.

In fact, as you read this book, you may be thinking to yourself, *Just tell me the punchline right now — I'm a busy person and don't have time to read a whole book*! If you are thinking these thoughts, it means that your own how/best mindset is being activated right now.

For argument's sake, how annoyed would you feel if I told you that the book does not include a summary of all the solutions up front, because, to embrace creative change, you have to understand what the strategies are and when to use each. This might mean that you have to carefully read the entire book. Now rate this level of annoyance on a 1–7 scale (1 = not at all, 4 = don't know, 7 = extremely so). If you gave yourself a rating above a 4, this could indicate that your how/best mindset is activated. This is certainly not a scientifically rigorous method; it is rather an exercise to help you develop more self-awareness about what kind of mindset you function in. In the chapters that follow, I will propose that knowing what mindset you are in — or better yet, *shaping* the mindset you are currently in — is the first step toward helping you embrace creativity rather than rejecting it outright. I will also provide you with exercises and ways of activating mindsets to help you self-disrupt, if you think you might be entrenched in a how/best way of seeing the everyday world.

For those of you who remain entrenched in your how/best mindset and want to get to the practical solutions as fast as possible, it is important to note that the answer to how you embrace creative change is not as simple as just having a why/potential mindset and moving on. Creative change is one of the most complicated psychological processes that exists, and it is tremendously difficult to learn. So there is no single life hack to make creative change. In fact, I will describe in more detail when a how/best mindset can actually *help* you embrace creative ideas, while an unchecked why/potential mindset can possibly lead you down the path of being overly optimistic about new ideas. That said, because creative change is so difficult to embrace, let alone enact, if you take the time to learn how to make creative change happen, you will have a rare and valuable skill that will differentiate you from your competition.

For now, though, it is important that you understand one basic idea: we *hate* uncertainty around creative ideas, but we also *love* it. Sometimes uncertainty around creative ideas can be energizing and interesting because it stimulates our curiosity — a state that most often happens when we are in the process of generating a creative idea.

But when we are evaluating whether a creative idea that we didn't generate can solve our own problems, there is more variability in how we experience uncertainty. We can experience hope and excitement about all the possibilities, but also anxiety and fear about potential failures. This also means that when you pitch creative ideas to others, you can help lead them down the path of feeling uncertainty, fear, and anxiety, *or* toward curiosity and hope. Whether you can make yourself or someone else feel hope rather than anxiety about a creative idea could be the key to your embracing and advancing creative change.

AREN'T DECISION MAKERS THE EXPERTS ON CREATIVE IDEAS?

If the process of evaluating a creative idea is a psychological one and not a rational one, this suggests something very important and powerfully positive. Just because someone is a teacher, or a CEO, or even a decision maker with power over you, they do not know with any certainty whether your creative idea is the one that will enhance any future outcome such as learning, safety, or profit. In fact, there is no known methodology in existence that can reliably and accurately pinpoint a newly formed idea's full potential.

This of course can be an extreme source of discomfort for decision makers.

This also means that if a decision maker calls you "naive" or "quirky," or says definitively that your new ideas won't appeal to others, it may merely be a defensive reaction to the anxiety your idea makes him feel. And best of all, this means that, in some ways, you are on an even playing field with those who have decision-making power. You and the decision maker are in the same predicament; neither you nor he can accurately predict the future.

After almost twenty years of researching this problem, I have come to realize that experts, doctors, decision makers, parents, and pretty much everyone else is floundering in confusion when it comes to vetting the future potential of creative ideas. When ideas are truly new (when they have never been presented or used before by you or others), it is very, very difficult to determine on the spot if a new idea will work in the future in a given situation. I believe that this very uncertainty, combined with a push to have accurate solutions now (the source of the how/best mindset), is at the heart of why people instinctively disdain creativity and decision makers think that whether or not an idea is creative is irrelevant to whether the idea is great and will solve problems.

The Science Behind the Paradox

MOST PEOPLE WON'T ADMIT THAT THEY HATE creativity. I have asked hundreds of people — executives, managers, workers, students — in the United States whether they think creativity is valuable. That is, I asked them to rate the extent to which they thought creativity was important and valuable on a 1 to 7 scale where 1 meant not at all important/valuable, 4 meant not sure, and 7 meant extremely important/valuable.

Guess what I found? An astounding 95 percent of people who took my survey said creativity was a 5 or above on the scale. Virtually no one gave creativity an importance rating lower than a 4.

I next conducted an intensive search on articles about creativity in the popular press, and I did not find a single article that said creativity was a waste of time. Not one. Not only that, but I found just one media piece among the hundreds that I looked at that asserted that creativity is naive or misguided.

I started to take notice of what CEOs said about innovation, which invariably included phrases like "competitive advantage," or "strategic advantage," or "edge over our competitors." In fact, I challenge you to find a single example of a CEO telling the media, "We do not want innovation. We do not care if our company offers customers creative solutions."

If you look at investor reports and company mission statements and strategic plans, around 20 or 30 percent will say something positive about innovation. You will never hear any business representative claim or read a company newsletter that says, "We don't want creativity here — that is not our job."

So even though people profess to love creativity, we know that creativity isn't all unicorns and rainbows. When you have to convince others to use a new idea and take a risk, all of a sudden the love affair ends. I've received so many emails from professionals telling me all the many different ways their creative ideas have been summarily and brutally rejected. So what could cause all these negative feelings about creativity, and why are they often hidden?

THE PARADOX OF EXPERTISE

The first time I recognized my own bias against creativity was when I was teaching a class on, ironically enough, creativity. I had divided my MBA students into groups and had them engage in a brainstorming task commonly used in experimental research on creativity. The task was to have groups generate as many unusual uses as they could think of for a simple cardboard box. These brainstorming tasks usually involve around ten minutes of idea generation, followed by five minutes for each group to choose their best idea to present to the class.

Now, as you can imagine, I've heard the gamut of unusual uses before — everything from using the box material to make high-fashion clothing to using the box as a house to live in. So I was a bit unprepared when one team presented their best idea, one they were so excited about that they asked me what I thought as soon as they had presented it. Their idea: a solar oven.

When they asked me what I thought of their idea, something strange happened that has never happened to me before. Before I could stop myself, I said, "A solar oven? That makes no sense at all!" If you have ever done or said something stupid, like I did that day, you might also have experienced what I did after my comment landed. Everything suddenly slowed down, and then three things happened. The first was that my brain asked me why I had publicly blurted out such a strong negative reaction to the idea. The second, I looked at all my students' faces; the students who had come up with the idea were understandably surprised, embarrassed, and uncomfortable. The third thing was that I tried to remedy my students' discomfort by saying something that, unfortunately, sounded even more judgmental: "Does anything like that actually exist?"

One student stepped forward and patiently explained to me that solar ovens were commonly used in India to cook food, and the box form was indeed a common type of solar oven. But since the use of a box as a solar oven was new to most Americans, it met the definition of *creative* by being both novel and useful.

I was surprised and slightly horrified by my knee-jerk and resistant response. I had publicly criticized an idea that was actually great. And I had done it automatically, without thinking, as a reaction to not knowing something that, to me, was truly new. Because I had not yet learned how the bias against creativity works, or why, I wasn't able to turn my poor response into a learning point. Instead I meekly dropped the discussion and moved on to the next topic.

As I looked back later on my odd behavior, two things struck me. First, I had scored extremely high on a scale called "openness to experience," which measures a person's general tendency to feel open to new ideas and to exploring them. So it made no sense to me that I — a theoretically highly open person who studies and loves creativity — could experience such a knee-jerk bias against creativity. Second, my reaction was so powerfully negative and happened so fast that I was hardly in control of it in the moment.

As I pondered what had caused my bias against creativity, I dug deeply into the academic literature to try to find answers. Sadly, the outcome of my deep dig made me feel pretty depressed. Academics all believe that expertise is the key to evaluating a creative idea. So by that measure, as an expert in creativity, I should be really good at evaluating creative ideas for a simulation I've run countless times, right? But since I clearly wasn't, I wondered if the problem was with me.

I thought, maybe evaluating a *creative* idea was a different kind of task than evaluating a *familiar* idea. Maybe having expertise when evaluating a familiar idea does make a lot of sense. In fact, when you evaluate a familiar idea, having real expertise is key. But could expertise make it harder to evaluate — and embrace — a creative idea?

Experts in every field of endeavor make catastrophic errors in judgment all the time. Hewett-Packard rejected Steve Wozniak's rough concept for the Apple II, a move that caused Wozniak to quit the HP job he loved and go to work for Apple full-time. Def Jam Records dropped Lady Gaga from its roster of artists, and today she is a megastar. Steven Spielberg's application to the University of Southern California's School of Cinematic Arts was rejected not just once, but twice. Dr. Seuss's first book was rejected by twenty-seven publishers for being too "silly and different."

When Andre Geim and Kostya Novoselov first submitted their three-page paper about graphene — a new type of carbon-based material said to have greater conductivity and a lighter weight than silicon — it was rejected by *Nature,* a prominent journal in the sciences, for not being "a sufficient scientific advance." The paper was instead published in *Science,* and Geim and Novoselov won the 2010 Nobel Prize in Physics. Clearly, the editor at *Nature* — surely an expert at determining which papers to accept and which to reject for publication — made a big mistake in this case and rejected the wrong paper.

These examples of creative ideas being rejected by experts — and many more just like them — are not flukes. One study looked at the three most prominent medical journals and found that they routinely rejected breakthrough papers in favor of papers with less novelty and impact. In fact, this study found that the journals in question rejected twelve of fourteen of the most important breakthrough papers published at the time. This means that editors read all fourteen breakthrough papers and disliked twelve of them so much that they didn't bother sending them out to reviewers for further consideration. This general pattern of findings has been replicated many times. Another study found that novel ideas had a higher likelihood of being rejected even if they were of high quality. One paper in my field found that the most novel papers were rejected from a prominent management journal — but this finding was so well established that this paper was itself rejected for not being a "sufficient scientific contribution."

Could experts be struggling when evaluating creative ideas? Laura Kornish at the University of Colorado Boulder and Karl Ulrich at the Wharton School collected data from a company called Quirky. The business model for Quirky encourages people to submit new ideas, to vote on which ideas they like, and then to vote on development decisions for specific ideas, which will then be commercialized and sold on the company's website. The researchers took a subsample of ideas from the Quirky website and had a panel of seven experts — as well as a group of ordinary consumers — rate their purchase intent based on the early-stage models of the ideas. What they found was pretty astounding.

First, the experts didn't agree with one another. Second, the expert ratings were not at all predictive of product sales, but the nonexpert consumer ratings were. In fact, a sample of four consumer ratings was just as predictive of product success as was a sample of four expert ratings. And all you needed were twenty consumer ratings to achieve significantly better predictive power than using a sample of experts. Another study found that a group of around forty indie moviegoers was far more accurate in predicting future box office returns than a group of thirty experts. What this suggests is that whatever experts know, it doesn't necessarily help them accurately evaluate something new.

A study conducted by Page Moreau, Donald Lehmann, and Arthur Markman found that, relative to novices, experts in film technology rated a digital camera (a new technology in 1999 when the study was conducted) as having low product viability. Further, film experts rated a camera with incremental novelty (i.e., a film-based camera with new flash technology) as highly viable relative to novices, who felt the incremental camera had little value.

Another study found that highly experienced venture capitalists made poor investment decisions relative to those with a moderate level of experience. Yet another found that venture capitalists' ratings of business viability for early-stage ventures did not predict whether these same ventures survived, grew, or were highly successful in the long term.

But how could this happen? Editors, professors, and business executives are experts — it is their job to recognize creative opportunity. So why do experts fail so often at making creative change?

WHY EXPERTS CAN STINK AT EVALUATING CREATIVE IDEAS

How could experts fail to recognize creative opportunities when they should be great at recognizing them? Shouldn't an expert know a lot about her field so she can easily pick out what's new and vet whether the new is going to be useful?

In his book *Zero to One,* Peter Thiel would seem to agree with this view. According to Thiel's approach, truly innovative ideas (like most innovation gurus, he does not use the term *creative*) are completely new — they go from 0 (never having existed) to 1 (existing). According to Thiel, if a product goes from version 1 to version 2 or even from version 2 to version 3, these kinds of changes are not "creative," not radical departures because they merely involve improving what exists. So according to this logic, if we are trying to recognize whether an idea is creative, then expertise in the 0 should help us pick out the 1, right?

In their study, Page Moreau and colleagues noted that experts were using what they knew about the 0 (i.e., film) as their reference point to evaluate the 1 (i.e., digital). Experts were concerned about digital cameras not requiring a darkroom, high-speed film, and specific exposures. To an expert in film, these things were baseline requirements for obtaining a quality photograph. Here is the problem: None of these things is a baseline requirement to obtain a quality photograph when you're using a *digital* camera. A novice might not even pick up on this point, but an expert would be acutely aware of the difference.

To an expert, a new product that does not require any of the basic features believed to be critical to product quality might seem questionable and of poor quality. In other words, experts are using the reference points they are expert in to determine whether an idea has features that are creative. Doing this is problematic because creative ideas can be a poor fit to existing paradigms or templates precisely *because* they are creative (e.g., digital cameras don't require darkrooms). In contrast, the novices — those who had no experience with film — thought the digital camera was great.

Ironically, knowing a lot about a reference point works wonders when evaluating a familiar idea. If you are an expert mechanic, you would probably know how to evaluate the engine in a 1969 Ford Mustang. You would know exactly what your reference point — a perfectly running 1969 Ford Mustang engine — looks like, sounds like, feels like, and even smells like. And you would know that any deviations from your reference point are things you'll need to fix.

But when it comes to creative ideas, it is more difficult to know how to interpret the quality of a new idea when it has features that differ so dramatically from our basic reference points. Even experts have little experience using, understanding, or thinking about an idea if it is truly new and different. So when it comes to new ideas, experts know less about how to effectively use reference points than they do when evaluating *familiar* ideas. Importantly, relative to novices, experts also know more about what they *do not know* — the unknown unknowns (e.g., what happens to picture quality when you no longer have a darkroom?). This means that when you evaluate something that is new, all your expertise does is help point out that you don't know anything about it.

This might explain why successful ideas — ideas that experts have vetted and liked — tend to strongly resemble the structure of existing ideas. For instance, the first railway passenger cars were based on the design of the stagecoach (without the horse). And then there's the caveman in *2001* who discovers how to use a bone as a weapon — one of the most radical innovations in the history of humanity. The caveman can see the link between his current definition of a weapon, his fist, and the new definition, the bone, because he views the bone as a different kind of fist. When people recognize a creative idea, the kind of novelty they are looking for is the kind they are familiar with. One reason for this may be that experts have more uncertainty to cope with when evaluating a new idea than a novice has. So one way to diminish this uncertainty is to see the familiar in the new.

Among Teresa Amabile's early work is a wonderful paper that explains why experts might devalue creative ideas. She conducted a laboratory study wherein subjects read positive and negative book reviews and then assessed the intelligence of each book review's author. She found that authors of negative book reviews were rated by participants as being more intelligent than authors of positive book reviews. This means that experts have less to lose and much to gain when being critical of new things, and more to lose when they embrace the new.

In other words, we don't recognize a 1 just because it is different from a 0. When we recognize creative ideas, we don't go from 0 to 1 at all. Instead, we go from 0 to a totally different kind of 0 (like the letter *O*). We recognize creative ideas because they are different from our reference points. *But the quality of this difference is key.* This difference has to fit our beliefs about what creativity looks like. Differences that are too big don't fit because they are unfamiliar and maybe even bizarre. Differences that are too small don't fit because they are boring and trivial. The difference has to be different enough, but also familiar enough for us to categorize it as creative.

THE NATURE OF OUR LOVE/HATE RELATIONSHIP
WITH CREATIVITY

Recognizing creative opportunity is all about *fit*. When something fits our definition, it no longer seems as uncertain and unsafe. This means that the psychological experience of fit influences how we feel. People love the experience of fit. When the world looks just as we expect it will, we feel safe — no reason for fear. Fit with our expectations influences our liking of: color swatches, paintings, and music. In contrast, when the world does not fit our expectations, that means something is wrong.

Feeling the fit gets tricky when we recognize creative ideas. By definition, creative ideas don't fit perfectly into existing paradigms and templates. For this reason, it is difficult to know if new ideas are useful, reliable, and so forth. So when you evaluate a creative idea, it's less likely you will feel this psychological experience of fit. This should mean that, on average, people should dislike creativity. But virtually no one in my sample did. When I told Teresa Amabile about this, she asked a pointed question: "Why do people say they love creativity?"

Why are people so quick to admit love and so hesitant to admit hate for creativity? We know that most cultures have extremely positive views of creativity. When children learn about American culture and history in grade school, they are exposed to the image of the rugged pioneer who rebelled, explored, and forged a new world in the Americas. And, in truth, the birth of the United States is a story of gaining the intellectual freedom to think differently. One of the major features of American culture is a strong focus on individualism — the extent to which a person is seen as distinct and unique from others. Hence, if American culture values uniqueness, and uniqueness is a distinguishing feature of creativity, it could be that saying you love creativity is about as socially mandated as saying you love America.

Also, people tend to love *their own* creative ideas. People describe the process of being creative as enjoyable, interesting, fun, meaningful, and challenging. One company I studied gave its employees a certain percentage of their workweek free to explore their own new ideas. An employee described this policy as "a perk, like taking a vacation in your mind from all the day-to-day monotony."

Furthermore, there is lots of evidence that when we label something as creative, it means that we like it. Jeff Loewenstein and I found that both Americans and Chinese said creativity made them feel joyous and inspired them with awe. Evidence shows that people who label products as creative want to buy them. When executives label something as creative, there are strong norms to endorse and to select the idea too.

There are clearly strong norms in favor of supporting creativity, but we also know that new ideas have a high failure rate. New ideas are buggy and rarely work perfectly the very first time you try them. We don't know much about new ideas relative to familiar ones. On average, people don't like the state of not knowing something. So there are lots of reasons for people to dislike creative ideas too. Because creativity can make us feel really bad, but we want to uphold cultural norms around saying creativity is great, we are in a bind. There are two ways our brains may decide to resolve this problem.

When the world tells us that our hateful feelings are wrong, we want to hide them from view. We can hide them by simply faking it and pretending to like something. We can also hide our negative feelings from ourselves. We can authentically think we love something that our unconscious mind hates. One leader I worked with volunteered to chair a committee to actively promote women in his organization. I believe his desire to increase the number of women in leadership positions was authentic. Oddly, however, when promotion time came, this same leader decided not to promote a highly qualified woman to a leadership role and hired a less-qualified man instead. This indicated to me that while he did have a positive, authentic regard for women, he might also harbor unacknowledged views that women are better suited for home life than work.

In either case, there is strong evidence that our implicit (or unexpressed) beliefs can be very different from our explicit (or expressed) beliefs, in part because there are such strong social norms and rules of appropriate behavior that govern what we tell others we think.

Could the bias against creativity operate similarly to the biases we have against certain groups of people? Just as people can express authentic positive feelings toward a given social group as well as strong negative implicit or unacknowledged feelings toward the same group, could we feel strong positive feelings toward creativity but then end up keeping our negative feelings under wraps — hiding them so as not to violate social norms?

When my colleagues Shimul Melwani and Jack Goncalo and I first searched for the bias against creativity, we were pretty doubtful that we would find it in an undergrad population. We figured that millennials love creativity.

We were right. When we ran the first studies, we found that millennials loved creativity — explicitly (because they told us they did) and implicitly (because their reaction times told us they did). We used a reaction-time test called the IAT — the implicit attitude test — commonly used when studying racial bias. The IAT assesses more automatic responses to word or concept pairings. So the structure of the IAT makes it harder for participants to fake their responses and present themselves in a socially desirable way.

The way we structured the IAT for creativity was to pit words associated with creativity against words associated with practicality. We then asked people to pair these words with words indicating good (e.g., *peace, cake, heaven*) or bad (e.g., *rotten, vomit, hell*). Faster reaction times pairing creativity-related terms with words like *peace* and *cake* and slower reaction times pairing creativity-related terms with words like *rotten* and *vomit* indicated a more implicit love of creativity.

But not all students were in love with creativity. When we examined mean ratings of explicit and implicit bias by undergraduate major, we found that engineering students explicitly said they loved creativity. But when it came to their implicit ratings, engineering students paired the words related to creativity with words like *rotten, hell,* and *vomit* more quickly than with words like *peace, cake,* and *heaven.* In fact, they paired words related to practicality more with *peace, cake,* and *heaven.* In short, we found our first evidence that people could say they loved creativity but implicitly show negative associations with creativity relative to practicality.

You might then wonder, could students who elect to go into engineering programs have personalities that are less open to experience, and therefore to creative ideas, than students in other majors? A good question, so in our study we asked people to fill out a questionnaire assessing their openness to experience, but statistically controlling for openness to experience did not diminish the extent to which engineering students implicitly hated creativity.

The overall point for our team was that the bias could be changeable or malleable. That is, instead of being something that people had or did not have as a trait, the bias could be something that situations (e.g., someone's choice of major) could evoke.

The first experiment we ran exposed participants to either a control condition or a risk-taking experimental task. In the control condition group, participants just filled out questionnaires unrelated to the study. In the experimental condition, participants were told to press a button to inflate a balloon on a computer screen. Every time they pressed the space bar, there were two possible outcomes: the balloon might inflate further, giving them a larger cash prize, or the balloon might burst, giving them nothing and ending the task. After they engaged in this exercise, we told the experimental group that, regardless of their performance, we would randomly assign one person in the study to receive a cash prize. Both groups — control and experimental — were then prompted to complete the explicit and implicit attitude tests.

Everyone in the sample, regardless of condition, explicitly said they loved creativity. That is, when we asked participants, "Do you value creativity?" they said, "Yes." But when we looked at the reaction-time test, it told a different story. In the control condition group, everyone associated creativity with *peace, cake,* and *heaven.* In the experimental condition group, where people felt uncertain, they associated creativity with *rotten, vomit,* and *hell.* Just as people can *express* positive regard for others in a certain social group while also harboring strong negative *implicit* feelings toward those same people, we showed that participants had strong positive expressed regard for creativity even though reaction-time tests showed that they associated creativity with words like *rotten, vomit,* and *hell.*

We also wanted to show how people's implicit bias against creativity would shift how they assess creative ideas. In a second experiment, we directly manipulated tolerance for uncertainty. We randomly assigned participants to one of two condition groups and prompted them to write about one of two statements: *For every problem there is only one correct solution* (this is the uncertainty *intolerance* prime — the first manifestation of the how/best mindset), or *For every problem there is more than one correct solution* (this is the uncertainty *tolerance* prime — the first manifestation of the why/potential mindset). We subsequently had participants take the creativity-practicality IAT and also rate an idea (i.e., a running shoe with nanotech that adjusts fabric thickness to reduce blisters) we had pre-tested that showed extremely high levels of creativity.

People primed with the how/best mindset explicitly told us they loved creativity but they implicitly associated creativity with words like *vomit* and downgraded the creative idea. People primed with the why/potential mindset also told us they loved creativity, but they associated creativity with *cake* and rated the creative idea highly.

Taken together, what we found is not just that people dislike novelty, which is what prior work had shown. Instead, we identified that people worshiped creativity — implicitly and explicitly — except when they felt uncertain. When they felt an intolerance toward uncertainty, they still weren't ready to openly admit that they disliked creativity, but their reaction times showed that they harbored automatic and potentially unconscious negative associations with it that led them to downgrade a creative idea. We get in this bind when we use a how/best way of viewing the world.

What does this mean for you? You, your boss, or your coworkers can say you love creativity, but at the same time, you may also hate it. Our negative feelings about creativity are tricky because we don't admit them. Instead, our negative feelings might be more automatic and even unconscious. In other words, you may not be aware that you harbor negative feelings for creativity.

WHY ARE YOUR GREAT IDEAS
GETTING REJECTED?

Chances are, if you're reading this book, you've developed a creative idea. And, chances are, given peoples' propensity to feel uncertain about creative ideas, your idea was rejected at least once. If that rejection hurt a lot, it was probably because the rejection came from a person with gatekeeping or decision-making power. We care very much whether gatekeepers embrace our creative ideas. Our ideas have a chance of making an impact in our organizations only if decision makers say *yes* to them. When gatekeepers say yes, it allows more and more people to see, use, and evaluate our ideas. When gatekeepers say no, we either have to find another gatekeeper or our creative ideas go into the file drawer, never to be seen again.

Organizations employ gatekeepers to coordinate how resources are allocated toward idea development and implementation. Many organizations have steering committees that govern which ideas are funded and which are not. For example, book publishers have acquisition committees that decide which book proposals are accepted for publication and which are not.

Most organizations employ gatekeeping roles to govern how they innovate. Product development companies, for example, might have layers upon layers of gatekeepers. In one company I worked with, to get an idea through, an employee has to pitch the idea to her manager. If the manager says yes, then the employee has to pitch the idea to the steering committee of higher-level managers. If that steering committee also says yes, then she has to pitch the idea to the regulatory folks (e.g., the legal department). If the regulatory department says yes, then she has approval to make a prototype. After the prototype is made, the whole chain of decision making starts all over again to get approval to mass-produce the product.

As you can see from this example, decision-maker roles are the key to ensuring that our ideas don't die an early death. But what if decision-making roles themselves were the problem? Could the very existence of the gatekeeper/decision-maker role kill creative-idea recognition? Regardless of what people know, what if adopting a decision-making role caused people to adopt a how/best mindset and to devalue creative ideas?

Shimul Melwani, Jeff Loewenstein, Jennifer Deal, and I wanted to know the answer to this question. We recruited undergraduate business majors and invited them into the laboratory. We showed participants a video of a professor describing trying out a new idea for a pitch-contest format by and for the students. We randomly assigned one group of participants to a decision-maker role and the second group to a control condition where they merely evaluated an idea.

For the decision-maker role, students were told that they were responsible for whether ideas were pushed to the next level, and they would be accountable for their evaluations being of good quality and how resources would be spent. For the control condition, we told students that their ratings, in aggregate, would determine whether an idea was pushed forward.

We then had all participants — regardless of condition group — rate an idea. The idea we used was pretty fun — it was dirty-diaper roofing, in which roofing materials are made out of dirty diapers through a process of thoroughly sanitizing and then manufacturing them into pellet form instead of disposing of them in a landfill. We showed everyone the same description of the idea, with one small exception — we included what some people might call *business viability data,* or even *vanity metrics.* Vanity metrics indicate the number of people in a crowd who endorse an idea (e.g., registered users, raw page views, number of downloads). One half of participants were told that the diaper-roofing idea received 22,000 Facebook likes and 178 percent of all requested funding from Kickstarter after a thirty-day campaign. The other group was told that the idea received just 22 percent of funding requested from Kickstarter investors after a thirty-day campaign, and only thirty-one Facebook likes.

What did we find?

First, decision makers had more of a how/best mindset than those in the control group. Further, decision makers, with their how/best mindset, thought dirty-diaper roofing was super-creative when it garnered lots of Facebook likes and Kickstarter investors, but not very creative when it didn't. Those in the control group, however, rated dirty-diaper roofing as super-creative, regardless of Facebook likes or investor funding. The funny thing was that decision makers didn't see the idea with lots of Facebook likes and investor funding as more useful than the idea with fewer likes and less funding, just more creative. And we replicated this finding using a different idea in a large Fortune 500 company in a sample that included CEOs.

By definition, creative ideas look different than familiar ideas proven by established paradigms. Creative ideas often don't have big market share, lots of investor interest, or Facebook likes — yet. There are many reasons for this. First, creative ideas are sometimes too early-stage and need some development or tweaks to appeal to consumers. Second, the ideas might not have found the right audience yet. And, as I'll discuss in Chapter 5, developers may have a terrific product but haven't yet learned how to pitch it properly to consumers.

The field used to believe that because creative ideas are often too new to have gained acceptance, it puts decision makers in a bind. Decision makers can choose a creative idea and risk their reputations should the idea fail, or they can choose a familiar, less-risky idea that might not solve the problem as well.

Except that we found that decision makers aren't really in a bind at all. They don't even see ideas with low social acceptance or poor vanity metrics as being creative in the first place. They only see the creative opportunity when ideas are highly accepted.

You might think this is reasonable. If ideas are highly accepted, aren't they going to succeed? Well, we know that Kickstarter investors can sometimes invest in an idea not because it's great, but because the idea has a great investor incentive structure (e.g., if you invest X amount, you get a cool T-shirt). And further, for a small fee you can *buy* Facebook likes — so these kinds of metrics are extremely easy to game and fake — one reason they are called *vanity metrics*. So even though these kinds of metrics are often unrelated to whether products are ultimately profitable, to a decision maker, they mean the products are creative. And these kinds of metrics have a second utility to decision makers. If a metric is great, then a decision maker can use that metric to justify why he made a decision to invest even though the idea later failed.

What do our findings mean overall? They mean that telling decision makers in your organization to embrace creativity is simply not enough. You can't overcome the bias against creativity by just saying, "Hey, choose creative ideas!" This is because people with a how/best view will shift their definition of creativity to suit their desire to reduce uncertainty and protect their own reputations.

This finding also means that decision-making roles can evoke a real bias against creativity. In most decision-making contexts, ideas with the highest scores advance to the next round. So in our experiment with business school undergrads, the mere fact that the diaper idea had fewer Facebook likes would have meant that it would not have advanced to the final round if the decision makers were in charge. But this same idea would have advanced to the final round if the evaluators — who did not have decision-making responsibility — were in charge. In other words, randomly assigning a student to a decision-maker role caused that student to devalue an idea that as an average person she would probably have loved.

We wanted to know the micro-mechanisms at work here. Why were decision makers devaluing an idea with low investor funding? It wasn't because they thought the idea was less useful, so what was it? Turns out, the answer is anxiety! When we primed people with a how/best mindset and they evaluated ideas with low investor funding, they felt more anxious about having to defend their evaluations to others. Those who didn't have a how/best mindset weren't anxious about defending their judgments of ideas with low investor funding at all.

Remember what I said earlier about experts having more to lose and less to gain by endorsing a creative idea? Well, the same could be true of people with no relevant expertise who are assigned to decision-maker roles.

So putting all the pieces together, we can see that experts often know things that make it harder for them to feel the fit. Experts may reject your great ideas because what they know about their reference points can make them more aware of what they don't know. But expertise — or what people know — is not the whole story. What you know matters, but your mindset also matters. Decision makers can reject your great ideas, too, and not because they aren't great. Our results show that assigning a decision-making role shifted creativity assessments even for ideas where participants had no expertise. The decision-making role evokes a how/best mindset and, very often, a reaction I call *the cover-your-butt response*. When decision makers have a how/best mindset, they will see creative opportunity *only* if the idea allows for them to cover their butts in case it fails. The number-one feature experts use to cover their butts is economic data.

Experts, and also decision makers with little expertise, will tell you, truthfully, that they love creativity. But the feeling of not knowing and the lack of fit occur often enough to make them feel anxiety and even hatred for creativity.

The organizational implications are concerning. If an organization employs decision-making roles to serve as the main gatekeeping function to resource ideas, it will struggle if it needs creativity to survive. Merely placing a person in a decision-making role can shift this person into a how/best mindset. Because people in how/best mindsets think of uncertainty only as a nuisance — they define great ideas as proven to have wide appeal. But new ideas aren't proven, by definition. Instead, ideas closer to the status quo have reliably proven metrics. For that matter, social approval metrics can be faked (e.g., Facebook likes or downloads bought from India). So even if you mandate that decision-makers select creative ideas, they will choose incremental ideas, or potentially bad ideas with fake social approval data. They will honestly believe both kinds of ideas are more creative than new ideas with relatively poor metrics. And if the ideas they choose fail in the marketplace again and again because creativity is needed, decision makers can use vanity metrics to cover their butts and keep their jobs. This kind of decision-making cycle can go on and on and contribute to an organization's uncreative destruction.

BIAS WARNING SIGNS

So what are the warning signs that can signal when we are biased against creativity (as opposed to negative but accurate in our idea assessments)? Unfortunately, there is no research on this topic yet, so I can only offer you my theorizing based on my own experience with the bias. For me, the first creativity bias warning sign is when we experience a strong, negative, knee-jerk reaction to an idea. So, instead of stimulating interest, questions, or curiosity — which are more reasonable responses to things we feel strongly about (positively or negatively) — the new idea immediately stimulates what I call an *ick response*. An ick response makes us want to move away from the idea and reject it outright instead of making us want to learn more about it.

Recently, a consulting client of mine had an ick response. A division in his company had developed a new way to sell an existing product, which he hated. When I asked him why he felt so strongly about the new idea, he said, "It just makes no sense to me, but I'm not biased against creative ideas — it's just that the idea is stupid."

When I probed further to figure out exactly why he didn't like the idea, he struggled to articulate why and ended up repeating, "It just seems silly and makes no sense." When he later found out that the department's idea had tested incredibly positively with audiences, he was bewildered and even more annoyed.

Breaking down his reaction, I would say that my client expressed extreme discomfort around feeling uncertain. He said he didn't understand the idea, and we know that this feeling of not knowing something is incredibly negative and can be aversive as well. For starters, not knowing something can feel like a threat to an individual's own identity as being smart or expert. For another thing, not knowing something suggests powerlessness or a lack of control. Not having control or power are states people uniformly hate. So it's not that the idea itself threatened my client. Instead, it was *how the idea made him feel* that threatened him.

The other piece of my client's reaction was to belittle the idea by calling it stupid. This piece could be the most telling creativity-bias warning sign of all because of the expression of contempt. That's a telltale marker that a person feels threatened. Contempt is a negative emotion that has a fascinating function; contempt conveys a person's perceived relative superiority to an object or a person.

So when my client called the idea stupid, he was implying that the idea was beneath him. Calling the idea stupid also distanced him from it — making it reasonable for him to ignore it. After all, why would you want to spend your limited time and energy learning about something you thought was beneath your notice?

The end result of a contemptuous remark is to show superiority relative to something — in this case the idea — which, from an internal standpoint, psychologically distances you from the source of the threat and, from an external standpoint, manages people's impressions of you as being "smarter" or "better" than the idea you are criticizing.

Shimul Melwani and I, along with Jen Overbeck at Melbourne University, published a paper showing that making a contemptuous remark toward your teammate made others on your team think you were smarter and more leaderlike, even when controlling for actual ability. We replicated this finding twice with undergrad and MBA student teams at two different business schools. This is why contempt is such a powerful marker of bias, because it provides a reason why a person can reject an idea with little thought or care, and it makes other people observing the reaction think that person is actually smart.

Of course, the irony is that the person rejecting the idea does not actually reject it because he is smart. Rather, he rejects the idea because he does not understand how to evaluate it. What he is really rejecting is the annoying sense of uncertainty that comes with an idea he doesn't understand. Learning how to distinguish between these two concepts — rejecting ideas versus rejecting the ways new ideas make us feel — is key to overcoming one's bias.

So what I have seen in others, and even felt myself, when experiencing this bias against creativity is a strong negative emotional reaction that compels people to immediately belittle the idea and then to shy away from it. When we feel this bias, our ick response keeps us from exploring the idea, from asking questions about and learning why we don't like it, and from learning what we might improve to make the idea better.

This means that we are more likely to reject creative ideas quickly and without much real thought, and that when we do reject creative ideas, we usually do so simply because we don't understand them and want to get away from that feeling of not knowing, because it makes us feel uncertain and unsafe. This also means that we might not reject creative ideas as readily when we think deeply about them first or have a dialogue with others who think differently than we do about them.

The first step toward combatting this bias against creativity is to become more aware of when we exhibit the bias warning signs. The second step is to learn how to transform these biased feelings into something that allows us to embrace the creative solutions that may ultimately enrich our lives.

To sum up, when you feel uncertain, find yourself intolerant to uncertainty, or are steeped in a how/best mindset, you may have knee-jerk reactions to reject the very solutions that could make your life better. Furthermore, other people are likely to feel the same way you do and to reject ideas they badly need when they are entrenched in a how/best way of seeing the world.

All this is important because if we are aware of the maladaptive way we have been managing our feelings about creative ideas, we can then regain some control over our ability to adopt creative change and learn to better cope with it. Once we recognize the implicit warning signs of resistance to new ideas, we can begin to develop strategies to overcome this negative response and turn it into something much more constructive.

Self-Disrupt: Overcome Your Own Bias against Creativity

IS ADOPTING A PURE WHY/POTENTIAL VIEW THE key to embracing great ideas that are also new? Intuitively, you already know the answer to that.

Nope.

Take the example of Better Place, dubbed by one *Fast Company* journalist as "the most spectacularly failed technology startup of the 21st century." Before 2014, the mission of Better Place was hailed (by its founders) as akin in importance to the invention of the light bulb, the steam engine, JFK's Apollo space program, the Ford Model T automobile, and the Internet. Savvy investors, including HSBC, Morgan Stanley, General Electric, and Vantage Point, bought into the founders' vision and together gave Better Place around $900 million in funding — an unheard-of amount of money for a company that was merely a concept.

What was Better Place all about? The company sold electric cars. What was the hype about? The hype was about *why* it sold electric cars, and the *potential* the company promised.

When, in 2010, I visited the Better Place Tel Aviv Industrial Park visitors' center, I had goosebumps. The center was elegant, with Apple-esque architecture — simple, modern, uncluttered; it was repurposed from the shell of an old oil storage tank. The first thing our guide told us when she started the tour was "Here, we aren't just about electric cars. Here, we are saving Israel — we are saving the world."

Then we were shown photos of company founder and savior Shai Agassi. The company's story begins in the mid-2000s with Agassi — then a rising star at enterprise software developer SAP — who had a vision while at Davos for the World Economic Forum. To emphasize this point, the guide showed us a clip of the TED talk Agassi had given in 2009, which our guide pointed out had received a long standing ovation. Agassi looked ruggedly handsome in his Steve Jobs–like black turtleneck, while telling the story of how, at Davos, he asked himself the question "How could you run a whole country without oil?"

The solution, he said, was to "convert a country to electric cars." The big *why* reason he gave for this solution was to "help end the auto industry's reliance on oil." The subtext concerned keeping Arab oppression, terrorism, and other threats from destroying the world. He hit this point home by saying that embracing his solution was about making ethical choices to save our economy — an aim akin to abolishing slavery, which, he noted, had jump-started the Industrial Revolution.

Our guide took us to a building dubbed a battery-swap station and addressed the main issues regarding drivers' fears of converting to electric cars. One main reason why people don't just go out and buy electric cars is because of range anxiety, or the fear that the car will run out of power before reaching a charging station. Another is that a conventional charging station can take several hours to charge a battery. So the way Better Place attempted to solve this problem was by creating battery-swap stations that would swap out a car's battery in about the same amount of time it takes to fill a gas tank — five minutes. The cars — manufactured by Renault — could drive 80 miles on a single, fully charged battery. So if you wanted to drive from Tel Aviv to the Dead Sea, which is around 90 miles, you would have to stop once for five minutes to perform a battery swap. Now all they needed to do was set up battery-swap stations in convenient locations all over Israel.

Shai Agassi's vision was hailed as an innovative paradigm shift that was going to create a massive disruption and eliminate the gas engine. Agassi looked the part of the conquering hero — he had the ear of celebrities, world leaders, and rich investors, he wanted to save the world, and he was fighting what might be seen as a common enemy. It was a pretty heady combination.

The problem was that he had no idea *how* to execute his plan.

Instead of starting lean, focusing on experimenting, and learning how to get the model right in Israel before rolling it out to other countries, Agassi immediately began a massive global expansion. This created so much of a coordination burden and was so complex that he needed to hire a management consulting group just to monitor it. He didn't hire people with expertise in the automotive industry, or people with real-world construction experience to build the swap stations. Instead, he hired people who had experience in high tech, and members of his family. And the cost of the company's cars wasn't actually as low as Better Place suggested ($20,000); prices climbed to $37,000 for the sedan itself plus $12,000 for the first four years' use of the charging station network.

When Agassi talked numbers — explaining how he could make his vision work — they just didn't add up. He said it would cost the consumer only $20,000 to buy the electric vehicle, and that owners would also have the option of installing a robotic arm in their garages for only $700 so they could perform the battery swap at home. Neither was true. Employees affectionately called these kinds of inconsistencies "Shai math." After all, the entire enterprise was so inspiring and intoxicating that these inconsistencies didn't seem to matter much. Investors must have felt the same way, because Agassi was still able to attract them even after the first numbers started to show fewer than estimated vehicle sales.

I believe that Shai Agassi was able to keep raising money amidst declining revenues and numbers not adding up because he was able to distract investors and even consumers with an incredible feeling of fit. The first thing he did was to frame the problem with a big *why*. It wasn't just any old why — it was a why that fit with all the other details: to end the auto industry's reliance on oil. The why fit with the way the visitors' center had been made from a repurposed oil storage tank. The why fit with the product, a novel technology. The why even fit with Agassi's image as an innovator (e.g., his dressing like Steve Jobs during his TED talk).

We fall in love when a big why beautifully frames a picture, making all the other details seem like a fit. Whys with fit can distract us from the many hows. Whys put you in a broader state of mind — making you consider higher-order categories of things — whereas hows put you in a much narrower state of mind, making you consider the details of things.

If you define Agassi's vision in more *how*-oriented terms, you might focus on the centerpiece of his vision — the car battery. You might think about the battery being owned, stored, recharged, and swapped out by Better Place, or the specific make and model of the battery, the overall amount of charge the battery has, and the cost of the battery to the company. If you are focusing on the battery, it is much harder to see how that fits into a system that relies on lots of battery-swapping stations in a country like Israel that has very little land left to build on. You might also get concerned about whether your swapping stations could handle different models of batteries, or what would happen if the battery technology and shapes changed, rendering your swapping stations irrelevant. A how/best mindset can create this uncertainty spiral that builds upon itself, making you feel more and more uncomfortable about an idea that is new. Said differently, unproven but new (i.e., merely novel) ideas don't fit a how/best approach that values a sense of certainty around feasible implementation.

If you define Agassi's vision in *why*-oriented terms, around reducing dependency on oil, then the car battery might not seem that interesting or even that important. And if the *why* is attracting other investors, then you might reasonably think that they know something you don't and worry even less about the details. And of course, you can use the fact that many high-profile investors lost money to justify a failed investment.

The problem with big whys is that they can inoculate us from caring about the many hows that are critical to success. When you are focusing on the belief that you are saving the world by embracing an electric car, for example, you aren't necessarily as worried about whether the business you are investing in has a sound implementation strategy. That's a real problem.

THE HOW/BEST ADDICTION

The first time I stepped into the MBA classroom as an instructor, I was a rookie, a newly minted PhD teaching a class on strategic human resource management (SHRM) at Yale School of Management. I was terrified. I wasn't sure what SHRM was, and I had no idea how to teach the class. My only experience with MBA teaching had been indirect, watching professors at Harvard Business School to glean some tips. Curiously, even though the professors I watched all had different styles and case materials, there was one common theme they all shared when teaching negotiations or leadership. They would say, "There are no right answers. Instead, there are multiple ways to effectively handle the same situation." So that's what I told students in my SHRM class. Imagine my surprise when they all nearly revolted.

SHRM is all about "best practices," they said — an idea that was news to me at the time. "Don't you know about best practices?" Later I came to understand that the term *best practice* is used in business to refer to an action that is widely adopted or adopted by a successful company or person. So if Google is doing it, in these students' minds, it is by definition a best practice. The fact that Google might change or revise ineffective practices is almost irrelevant, because from the best practice perspective, if they were doing it once, there must have been a good reason why.

The best practice approach is one marked manifestation of a how/best way of thinking about solving problems. Unfortunately, it is also a blatant manifestation of what scholars have termed the *status quo bias*. People have an irrational preference for the status quo over equally good but newer options. If a policy or procedure already exists, we like it more than an untested procedure even if we have never seen it before. And if something has existed for a while and is used by many, we assume it's great, because we believe in survival of the fittest.

People can get addicted to a how/best mindset because it helps them have great confidence in decisions that require very little cognitive effort to make. There is also a second benefit for adopting a how/best way of thinking. If someone says that his company's policy is a best practice, it makes that person seem more expert and in the know, and it can allow him plausible justification for his actions if he fails. So if an entrepreneur justifies a failed action by saying "Well, it worked for Google," it might seem less like the entrepreneur was just ignorant. In other words, it seems like a solid defense, even when it may not be.

The best practice approach is only one manifestation of the

kinds of thinking reinforced by a how/best mindset. But the fact that it is so prolific and widely held can at least begin to give you a sense of how deeply rooted we can be in our how/best way of approaching the world. This of course gives rise to a key question: if the why/potential mindset can seduce us to embrace poorly executed ideas, but the how/best mindset activates our feelings of anxiety about new ideas, how do people embrace new ideas without knowing whether they are useful?

HOW TO SELF-DISRUPT AND MAKE CREATIVE CHANGE (WITHOUT FALLING IN LOVE WITH IDEAS OR REJECTING THEM OUT OF FEAR)

So, now that we better understand the nature of our own inherent bias against creativity, what exactly can we do about it? Fortunately, a lot. In the sections that follow, I'll describe a process I've developed to help you on your path to self-disruption.

Is there is a way to keep our love of novelty and concern about usefulness in check when evaluating creative ideas? I believe the answer is actually simple — create a *balance*. Not just why/potential, or how/best, but both. Let me explain.

Thomas Fogarty — the famous investor, physician, and entrepreneur — has designed more than 125 patents, won several industry awards, and led many medical-device companies to resounding successes. He has numerous inventions to his credit, including self-expanding stent grafts for aortic repair, a minimally invasive device for breast cancer diagnosis and therapy, and many others.

Dr. Fogarty learned about the challenge of making creative change at an early age. His father died when he was eight years old, which meant that his mother had to find work in a sweatshop to support the family. To help out with the family finances, at the age of fourteen, he got a part-time job at the local hospital for 18 cents an hour, cleaning hospital rooms and bedpans. He was later promoted to a position as scrub technician for a man who was to become his longtime friend and mentor, Doctor Jack Cranley.

When not working at the hospital, Tom invented things. He worked on model airplanes and rebuilt motor scooters, which he would then sell to the neighborhood kids. He was also a poor student, but thanks to his neighborhood priest and Dr. Cranley's recommendation, he was admitted to Cincinnati's Xavier University on probation.

Thomas Fogarty worked as Dr. Cranley's technician at several different hospitals, and this gave him a bird's-eye view of the many kinds of processes and procedures different doctors used. It was there that he learned the best practices of the day (circa the 1950s) around dealing with blood clots in limbs. Doctor Fogarty explained to me that, at that time, if you had a blood clot, there were only two procedures a doctor could do to save you. The first procedure — which had around a 100 percent failure rate — involved trying to scrape the clot out with forceps after opening up the artery via a very large incision. The second procedure was to amputate the limb. This meant that 50 percent of patients with blood clots died, and those who survived had to live without an arm or leg. Dr. Fogarty thought there must be a better way.

In his first year of medical school, Dr. Fogarty began to experiment in his attic. He took a urethral catheter and played around with the idea of attaching a balloon to the end of it. He created the balloon from the pinky fingertip of a surgical glove, and he used techniques he had learned fly fishing to tie the balloon to the catheter. His idea was that a surgeon only needed to make a small incision to push the catheter through the artery. The catheter could be pushed through the blood clot itself, at which point you could expand the balloon to the size of the artery walls, using saline. This would allow you to withdraw the balloon and clot through the artery via a small incision.

When Dr. Fogarty ran the clinical trials for his invention, he was delighted that there were no deaths and no amputations — all of his patients survived, with limbs intact. He wrote a paper to document his revolutionary success and submitted the manuscript for publication. Dr. Fogarty's balloon embolectomy catheter remains the gold standard of care and has saved millions of lives.

Dr. Fogarty is an inventor, but today, he also funds other inventors. Dr. Fogarty heads up the Fogarty Institute of Innovation. When I referred to his institute as an incubator for burgeoning medical-device companies, he railed in annoyance. "I hate that term. I think it gives people the false impression that all the companies in this collective are like eggs that will hatch and eventually walk. The reality is that nobody knows if any of these companies will ever get on their feet. Innovation is unpredictable."

I was intrigued by his response, and so I asked him, "If innovation is unpredictable, then how do you decide which companies to invite to the institute?" His eyes sparkled in response to my question. "Innovation is a process, a process that one does not learn in school, but from somebody encouraging you. When we teach, we don't encourage people to come up with new solutions. When you are teaching someone, you are trying to get them to think like you do. If you think of yourself as a teacher, then your students who come up with something new and different are out of line and disobedient, because, by definition, they didn't learn what you wanted them to. But when you encourage someone to learn, then you help them ask questions like *why* doesn't it work and *how* can I make it work better than it does now? You encourage them to come up with their own answers — even if you don't happen to know what the answers are yourself."

He continued, "I want to invite companies that have a solution that can benefit the patient, and I want company founders to learn how to make their products work in a timely fashion without wasting money."

I asked Dr. Fogarty to tell me in more concrete terms how he recognizes truly creative ideas. His reply: "A lot of what I do is gut feel. Some things are unconscious. But the truth is that I just don't know whether a company will be a creative success. I feel like I have to have all the answers, and that can make me feel anxious about things, so to calm myself down I tell myself, 'I could be wrong,' and I accept the fact that I might lose money. That happens every day."

SELF-DISRUPT: EVALUATE LIKE AN INVENTOR

What does *self-disruption* mean? I've heard this term used by lots of investors, executives, and even entry-level employees. Silicon Valley is obsessed with self-disruption. I've never heard it defined, although it is used synonymously with generating a creative idea or with taking a different path. I'll tell you what I think it means: self-disruption is the process of evoking creative change in oneself.

There are two ways you can self-disrupt when evaluating an idea. The first is by bringing to light all the definitions you have about the product you are evaluating and then actively challenging or expanding them yourself. This means that you would need to write down all your assumptions and beliefs about a product — even if they seem obvious — and then question each in turn, trying to find evidence to the contrary. I can tell you that I've never seen this kind of self-guided disruption actually work, which doesn't mean it *can't* work. On average, though, people on their own are just too resistant and stuck in their own definitions.

There is a second way to self-disrupt, which I also think is difficult, but less so than the first. This second form of self-disruption is what Dr. Fogarty practices. He uses his expertise to find the flaws in an idea, and to vet the quality of the founder. He uses his expertise to evaluate whether a device will benefit the patient. But once he has this evaluation in his sights, there is also a second step. He has to interpret this evaluation. He has to use a lens or a mindset to help him understand the meaning of all the facts. And he can actively choose to shift his mindset. Dr. Fogarty described this active choice when he said, "I feel like I have to have all the answers, and that can make me feel anxious about things." But then he says, "so to calm myself down I tell myself, 'I could be wrong.'" This kind of shift is Fogarty self-disrupting — he is disrupting how he is interpreting the information he has.

Mindsets are like computer programs that tell you how to interpret information. The how/best mindset is a program that tells your brain to reduce uncertainty. If there is something you are unsure about, one way to reduce that uncertainty is to tell yourself that any source of uncertainty sucks. The why/potential mindset is a program that tells your brain to tolerate uncertainty. So if there is something you feel uncertain about, you might reserve judgment or feel hopeful. Either mindset is too extreme to allow for a balanced view of an idea.

What is Dr. Fogarty's mindset? He doesn't seem to have a pure why/potential view. He cares about patient benefit, but the hows are also important — like how to make an invention work. Dr. Fogarty doesn't seem to have a pure how/best view either. Instead, as a lifelong inventor, he frames investment decisions in the way an inventor thinks. The definition of an inventor is someone who uses a process to learn how to make a new idea work. According to Teresa Amabile, the invention process starts with finding a problem, gathering information, generating options, testing the options, validating a solution, and then starting again if you fail.

The typical decision maker, though, might adopt a very different process than the process of invention. According to George Day at the Wharton School, decision makers should make a yes-or-no call by assessing the overall risks, using a careful and deliberate means of establishing a product's value to the company right now. This involves assessing a number of factors, including market size, profit margins, switching costs, feasibility of producing the product, the product's advantages over competitor alternatives, sustainability over time, fit with overall strategy, and so forth.

But do you have to think like a decision maker when evaluating ideas? Could you instead just think like an inventor? Could thinking like an inventor help you overcome this bias against creativity that can operate beneath your awareness? I think it can — and I have evidence that it does.

I know you want to rush and self-disrupt right now. But you aren't ready yet. First, if you have a strong how/best way of thinking, disrupting your mindset to think like an inventor will feel very uncomfortable for you. How/best mindsets are very sticky — and difficult to disrupt. Even if you don't have a strong how/best view, you need to prepare. What follows is a four-step process, along with a lifeline fifth step in case the four before it flop.

THE PATH TO SELF-DISRUPTION

Step 1: Identify whether you are evaluating familiar ideas, creative ideas, or both

Dr. Fogarty has the luxury of examining only creative devices. He doesn't evaluate the mundane, everyday stuff and then switch to evaluating the radical. This means that he can stay in his inventor mindset fairly constantly. He might need to keep himself from devolving into thinking like a decision maker, but that's easier than switching back and forth between thinking like a decision maker and thinking like an inventor.

The wisdom of crowds (WOC) for creativity. Your first task is to identify whether you are evaluating ideas that are high quality but either incrementally creative, radically creative, or both. This is not a trivial step.

How do you know if an idea is radically or incrementally creative? Some scholars just measure the creativity of an idea — if the creativity is high, then the idea is radical. If the idea has a low level of creativity, then it is incremental. So you could rate the kinds of ideas you evaluate on a 1–4 scale where 1 is not at all creative, 2 is slightly creative, 3 is moderately creative, and 4 is very creative. I like this scale because it forces people to truly decide whether something is creative or not. It will also give you a smidge of variance to work with, so if your creative ideas are all rated at close to 4, and your familiar ideas are all rated at 1, then you can make a strong case that these groupings of ideas are distinct.

What I'm recommending is a variation of the wisdom of crowds (WOC) approach. WOC is a technique that employs a crowd — meaning a large number of judges — to rate each idea, reducing error and increasing estimation accuracy. The way it works is that you provide any number of judges (your crowd) with a short description of several ideas (maybe a set of twenty or thirty ideas per judge). After you have at least twenty independent judges rate each idea, then you aggregate all the ratings, taking an average or sum for each idea. Then you rank the ideas on a bar chart to see which is above and which below the mean. If you used a brainstorming tool, you might generate several hundred ideas. So the wisdom of crowds could help you winnow through ideas relatively quickly and with greater accuracy.

Karl Ulrich at the Wharton School created a web-based tool called the Darwinator, which allows companies to employ crowds to evaluate large batches of ideas. I highly recommend using a tool of this sort. Most of these types of tools will ask people to rate the *quality* of the ideas (e.g., the value of a product to consumers, or consumer interest in a product), which I think is a great approach. But if you wish to self-disrupt, it is essential to rate the *creativity* of each idea as well.

In other words, I suggest you ask your crowds to rate each idea in your set on creativity *and* quality. (You can adapt the four-point scale above for the quality rating.) That way, you can see which ideas are of low quality and throw them out, but keep all your high-quality ideas. Of course, once you have these ratings, your job still isn't done. Just because an idea is of high quality and your customers want it doesn't mean you'll want to select it. You need to reserve judgment to assess whether the idea is or could be feasible, cost-effective, a strategic fit, etc. The point of WOC is merely to make the idea glut and subsequent idea-management problem a bit easier.

A word of caution when evaluating the creativity of an idea: Our work shows that people can very strongly disagree about what they perceive as creative. If you have a strong how/best decision-maker view, you might not be the best person to determine whether an idea is highly creative or not. And you might not even be the best person to rate the quality of highly novel ideas either. If you don't think an idea is feasible to begin with and not likely to be profitable, then to you it isn't creative or of high quality; in fact, it's dumb. We also have some evidence to suggest that you might view highly feasible ideas as incredibly creative, even though your customers don't. If you are in this boat, I suggest that you do not rate ideas yourself nor give them to your fellow decision makers to rate. Instead, give ideas to employees — those in idea-generator roles — or trusted customers to evaluate via WOC. Then aggregate your ratings to create an average creativity and quality rating for each idea. You can then use these creativity evaluations to group all high-quality ideas into two piles: ideas with high levels of creativity and ideas with low levels of creativity.

Develop an idea-evaluation plan. Now that you have two piles of ideas — or realize that you have only one pile — you know a lot more about the challenges you face. If you have one pile, and the ideas in it are all incrementally creative (below the creativity score of 3), then there's no need to self-disrupt. Assessing risk for these ideas makes a good deal of sense. If you have one pile and they are all highly creative, then you are in luck — you don't need to switch back and forth between self-disrupting and not having to.

Instead, you can go directly to the next step in the chain of self-disruption — Step 2 below. If, however, you have the misfortune to have two lovely piles of ideas — creative and not creative — then your road is going to be a bit tougher. If this third possibility is your reality, then you might consider several factors before sitting down and making your decision.

One recommendation is to place the familiar ideas and the creative ideas into two piles and to find two separate times to evaluate each kind of idea. Because evaluating familiar ideas is less mentally taxing than evaluating creative ones, you can plan to evaluate the familiar ideas whenever it makes sense. And because evaluating creative ideas might take a while and is mentally demanding, you might need to plan a bit more carefully for evaluating them. Practically speaking, try to schedule to vet creative ideas when you are well rested, not hungry, mentally alert, and feeling excited about the challenge.

If you are working in a group and have no choice but to look at all the ideas together, you might schedule your meetings to start with the creative ideas and then move to the familiar ideas later. One group I studied that had wonderful success with this strategy started with their most creative and hardest idea. Because they couldn't agree (which is common when it comes to creative concepts), they tabled the decision and moved to a more familiar idea. During the course of the meeting, however, the group intermittently cycled back to discussing their first creative idea while discussing other ideas on their list. Even though the members weren't officially discussing the creative idea, their thoughts about whether the idea made sense were developing, and they could compare that idea to other options over the course of the meeting without having to make a firm decision right away.

This is part of a process known as *incubation,* or the working of the unconscious mind. Our unconscious mind is believed to be much more efficient at finding associations than our active, deliberative thought processes. So even though this group tabled the discussion of their first creative idea, they were still making progress on it because each person at the meeting was incubating her thoughts on it while discussing other things. So, when it comes to discussing a creative idea, address it first, but reserve final judgment until the end of the meeting — even if you think the decision is a slam dunk — to give people time to let their thoughts incubate.

Step 2: Prepare to self-disrupt

We have a tendency to be anchored in the way we think. For example, in one rather entertaining study, researchers showed radiologists a lung scan and asked them to evaluate the scan for cancerous nodules. Unbeknownst to the radiologists, the researchers altered the scan slightly. They put a small but clearly visible waving gorilla in the far right-hand corner of the scan. Guess how many of the radiologists saw the gorilla? Only 17 percent! Eighty-three percent failed to see a waving gorilla on a lung scan. The radiologists were looking so hard for patterns they expected to see, they missed a pattern they didn't expect to see.

This could also mean that when you're looking for something you don't expect (like a creative idea), using pattern-finding activities can obscure your ability to find what you are looking for.

Perhaps this is why entrepreneur and venture capitalist Jordan Cooper noted, "The bottom 70 percent of VCs [venture capitalists] just go down a checklist [when evaluating new companies]: Monthly recurring revenue? Founder with experience? Good sales pipeline? X percent of month-over-month growth?" In other words, the *least* successful VCs' best practice is to simply pattern match.

But before you jump in and start evaluating something, take a quick break to prepare. First, check in with yourself. Notice how you are feeling now. What are you thinking? Are you worried about looking dumb in front of your boss or wanting to impress others? Just take a moment to notice where you are — so you can calibrate.

Think of an inventor you admire (maybe you). Give yourself an image that you can take with you when you evaluate an idea. Did you know that if you subliminally prime a person with pictures of the elderly, he will move slower and display poor memory? This is called *behavioral priming.* We all have beliefs about categories of people, so when these beliefs are activated, our behaviors follow.

For this reason, I'm suggesting that you prime yourself before you evaluate ideas. Bring to mind an image, stereotype, story, or memory of an inventor you truly admire — it can even be you. All you need to do is bring this inventor image to mind. Doing so will activate a whole host of other beliefs, like "think different," perhaps, or "quirky is good."

When you think of this inventor, also think of the invention you admire her for. Did this invention spring forth fully formed and looking perfect? Probably not. There were likely times when the invention didn't look so good, or there were serious hurdles the inventor had to overcome to make the idea work.

Think of a problem you are passionate about solving. Inventors usually have a big, overarching problem they care about solving. For Dr. Fogarty, it is patient benefit. For Mark Zuckerberg, CEO of Facebook, it's making the world open. For Herb Kelleher, former CEO of Southwest Airlines, it's enabling more people to fly. I'm not talking about mission, although your company's mission is important. And I'm not talking about making money, although making money is important too. I'm talking about a singular problem in the world you care about, or even a problem you have that the ideas you are about to evaluate might solve.

After you think of an inspiring inventor and reaffirm the problem you want to solve, check in with yourself one more time. Chances are you might feel a bit more hopeful, positive, and interested in the task ahead. If you still feel a bit negative or uncertain, you might try one more strategy: meditate. Meditation can improve your mood and also diminish cognitive biases.

Now you are ready to evaluate some creative ideas and disrupt your thinking.

Step 3: Self-disrupt—accept the unknowable

Would you be stressed out if your boss told you to send her a report every day on the previous day's company stock price? Probably not. You know how to check the stock price.

But would you be stressed out if your boss told you to send her a report every day on *tomorrow's* company stock price? If your company was in a stable market with few fluctuations, you might not know the exact answer but you might feel pretty confident that today's price would not differ significantly from tomorrow's. But what if the company was in a completely unstable market with wildly unpredictable fluctuations? I'm pretty sure your stress level would skyrocket. Why? Because you'd have an impossible task to perform. The more data you tried to gather about today's stock price, the more you would realize that there are just too many unknowns to predict what will happen tomorrow. And with creative ideas, this is a reality you always have to confront.

Accept that metrics today cannot tell you the future. When it comes to unknowns, you lack control over knowing the answer. If you have more than one unknown in an equation, calculating risk just isn't possible. Because of this, with creative ideas, calculating risk can truly be a waste of time. You can ask how big the market is for the product, and you might get an answer today. But if the inventor pivots the next day and decides to market the product to a different group, your carefully crafted answer becomes moot. If the inventor improves the idea or changes the way consumers use the idea, then the time, effort, and money you spent to generate the estimate was utterly wasted.

If an idea is in an early stage, metrics can be especially misleading. One study found that business viability data collected early in a new venture's history didn't predict later success. For example, the investors on *Shark Tank,* the popular TV show where entrepreneurs pitch their ideas to investors (sharks) in the hopes of getting them funded, passed on an investment in CBS Foods, a company that later became wildly successful. When passing on the opportunity, one of the sharks said, "Everything about you is right except for the numbers." So hardcore metrics can sometimes lead you down a path that doesn't accurately reflect the future value of an idea. Not only that, but using metrics to measure the unknowns may put you in the position of trying to achieve an impossible goal. When our goals are blocked, it causes us stress and anxiety, and it harms our health.

Decades of research have shown that the number-one way to increase your feelings of anxiety and negative emotion is to actively think about areas in your life where you lack control. One of my favorite studies in all of social psychology was conducted by Sonja Lyubomirsky and Susan Nolen-Hoeksema. They showed that when worried people were told to think about the source of their anxiety, they felt more anxious and depressed than when told to think about the face of the *Mona Lisa*. After reflecting on the face of the *Mona Lisa*, anxious people who came into the lab actually felt better. In other words, they could control their conscious efforts to think about the famous painting. But when they thought about those aspects in their life that they couldn't control, they became upset.

So the more people think about the things they cannot control, the worse they feel. Along those lines, if you decide to embrace a creative idea, there's a good chance that the metrics will make you feel nervous because they will remind you that you have no control over whether the idea will ultimately succeed. The solution here is to accept what you cannot know. If you are worried about generating profits, and the finger is pointing at you, do yourself a favor. Do a Fogarty. Take a deep breath and say, "I can't know the answer; nobody can know the answer; this is all a process." Accepting the unknowable (as opposed to trying to control it — an impossible goal) will improve your stress level and health.

Go with your gut. The best news for you is that accepting the reality that new ideas are unknowable can also help you make money. Laura Huang at the Wharton School and Jone Pearce at the University of California, Irvine, published a groundbreaking study showing that business viability data did not help angel investors choose better investments or big wins. What helped investors choose winning ventures was using their gut feel to make investment decisions.

What is investor gut feel? Gut feel is the positive impression you have of the person pitching the idea.

One investor in their study said, "You don't need to avoid uncertainty . . . the truth of the matter is that nobody is certain. I really feel like part of my success is being the person who says, 'It's okay. Be uncertain. Bear the uncertainty. Embrace it. Go with it. Let that lead you to the interesting stuff.' That's how I make my huge profits." In other words, when investors accept the unknowable, in addition to feeling better, they also become rich.

I asked Dr. Fogarty what "going with your gut" meant for him. He said that he has a sense for whether the founder can learn, is flexible, and is committed to making the device work.

You might wonder if I'm recommending that you throw metrics out and just not use them. My answer is a definite no. I think metrics are critical. The first step is to accept that the true metric is unknowable, and that metrics in the moment cannot tell you the true potential of an idea. This will help you manage your anxiety and go with your gut.

Step 4: Self-disrupt — shift from problem finding to problem solving

What does a metric actually mean? If you have a how/best mindset, you might use metrics to help you find problems or pinpoint red flags. Now think of that inventor you admire. How would he or she interpret a metric showing an idea's weakness? An inventor who knows that problem metric might actually use it to help improve the idea. In other words, inventors use metrics all the time, but they don't think of metrics as portraying the quality of an idea so much as giving them a clue about where ideas need to improve.

In short, how/best mindsets view metrics as *indicating what is*. Inventors view metrics as indicating *progress toward what could be*.

Frame constraints as problem-solving opportunities. If you were an investor in the mid-1990s and were deciding whether or not to fund Pixar's first movie, *Toy Story*, you would have had serious concerns about whether Pixar could deliver. The metrics (e.g., past performance indicators, profitability, product feasibility) were pretty awful. When Disney first funded Pixar to make movies, Pixar had never made a feature-length movie before. Before that deal was made, Pixar was losing a lot of money on their software business, so they didn't look great on paper. At the time, Steve Jobs was at the helm of Pixar. NeXT — the company Jobs tried to build after leaving Apple — was failing, and he was burning through cash fast. Former NeXT financial officer Susan Barnes described Jobs as a spendthrift. Brent Schlender and Rick Tetzeli, the journalists who wrote *Becoming Steve Jobs*, noted that, at the time, Jobs was starting to gain a reputation as a has-been.

At the time Pixar first started working on *Toy Story*, the software they had developed wasn't sophisticated enough to render faces without making them look plastic, not at all lifelike. Even if they could figure out how to make a human face look real, it was cost-prohibitive to include more than a few shots of a human face in the film. So how do you make a movie about the relationship between a boy called Andy and his toys without showing the boy's face?

The answer for Pixar was to show Andy's face only sparingly. Instead, we see a focus on the toys' faces and Andy's hands moving the toys. In later scenes, the viewer hears people speaking, but the action is shot from the perspective of the toys on the floor or in a different room. So while you hear the people talking, you only see their hands and legs or you see them from behind; you rarely their faces. But what I found truly startling was that the decision not to show human faces did not at all detract from the story. Instead, this decision only added to the movie by better showing events from the toys' perspective, the toys' story.

When you are in a problem-finding mode, feasibility constraints and failures are nothing but a red flag. But if you adopt a problem-solving way of viewing constraints, then suddenly you can frame the constraints as an important and challenging part of the problem you want to solve. Any inventor knows that constraints are real, but they don't stop the process of invention simply because they exist. If they did, nobody would ever invent. New ideas are rarely smooth sailing.

In a study Jeff Loewenstein and I conducted we asked people how they defined creativity. Seventy percent of Americans we questioned said creative ideas usually lacked feasibility, ease of use, and social acceptance. Seventy percent also said that those who develop creative ideas don't often have established reputations. Furthermore, most studies show that the more creative an idea is, the less feasible it is. It makes sense that when you are trying to do something you have never done before, you don't often have the immediate resources, skills, and knowledge to do it.

Lead the process, not the outcome. If you really do want creativity, it's best to accept that creative ideas may look pretty awful at first. But that doesn't mean that ideas can't improve. By adopting an inventor's perspective to evaluate ideas, you are in a unique position to provide guidance. You can provide guidance, though, only if you reserve judgment and give the idea generators a chance.

If you care about self-disrupting your how/best view, then focus on the image of the inventor you have in your mind — and think of yourself as a fellow inventor. Help the people whose idea you are evaluating to invent. Your perspective might be critical to the success of the idea, because idea generators may not be aware of all the constraints and feasibility concerns. Knowing the constraints sooner can help them waste less time, and as a decision maker, you might have access to better data about constraints. Setting guidelines like "We can't spend more than X" or "The product can't cost the consumer more than X" can help provide the idea developers with real direction without harming their creativity. There is a good amount of research showing that if you give idea developers a moderate number of constraints and guidelines, they can develop higher-quality creative solutions. In other words, instead of allowing metrics to slow or shut down the conversation, use metrics to provide the designers with clear and measurable guidelines to help them better understand the problems they are trying to solve.

If you have a how/best view, then showing certainty indicates to others that you know what you are doing. Saying "this cannot work," or even "this can work" in the context of vetting a creative idea makes you look confident and more leaderlike. But saying "We need to figure out how to make it work" implies that you don't know how to solve the problem and makes you look like less of a leader.

This is the main challenge of mixing and matching the process of evaluating familiar and creative ideas. When it comes to evaluating familiar ideas, experts really should be able to reliably predict if the solution will work or not. When it comes to evaluating creative ideas, expertise is still key, but it has limits. Expertise can tell you what needs to improve, but not whether your suggestions will guarantee that improvement. And expertise can help people become more aware of what they don't know. If leadership roles are granted to those who know answers, then being more expert may make leaders actually feel more anxious and less leaderlike, because they realize what they don't know.

For this reason, you could be concerned that problem solving (as opposed to problem finding) might make you look less leaderlike in the eyes of others. The good news is that when I see decision makers solve problems, they look even more leaderlike. In one meeting I observed, a decision maker said, "I know that all of you want to know the answer here. But I'm not convinced by any of this data. Because this is so new, let's give the designers a bit more guidance about how to approach the next steps."

Decision makers who adopt a problem-solving (versus problem-finding) frame quickly realize that they can present a different kind of expertise. You don't need to accurately evaluate an idea to be seen as a leader if you can lead the process itself. You can show leadership by setting guidelines and keeping inventors on track toward achieving them. You might even tell your team that you think of the decision-maker role as a kind of leadership role; it's the decision maker's job to encourage the project's direction, but not to know the answer before the team finds it. And when adopting this role, you might find yourself in the situation of having to manage others' anxiety about not knowing the answer. Remember, helping others accept the unknowable is a good place to start.

There is good evidence to suggest that idea developers benefit from good outside guidance. Even Steve Jobs lost his way when immersed in designing a computer workstation at NeXT. The workstation was supposed to cost just $3,000 but ended up costing closer to $10,000. In this case, Jobs would have greatly benefited by having a decision maker guiding his efforts and pushing back on design decisions that would ultimately price the workstation out of market range and cause it to fail.

But let's imagine you have tried all these steps. You have med-itated, you have accepted the unknowable, and you have tried to problem solve. But the how/best computer program in your brain is just too habitual. You just don't feel comfortable with not know-ing, and you can't make yourself problem solve when you clearly see the flaws. If, after all this, you still truly care about making cre-ative change, there is still hope. In fact, I suspect this is actually the path that most of us will need to take. The Dr. Fogartys of the world are rare for a reason: self-disruption is difficult. So if you are in this boat, don't worry. There is another very effective way to disrupt your thinking, though you won't be doing the disrupting. To disrupt your thinking using this method, you'll need help from someone else.

Step 5: Partner with your opposite

If you are a why/potential kind of person, pair yourself with a how/best kind of person to complement you, and vice versa. What I'm suggesting is that you structure the decision-making task so that there are two decision makers with distinctly opposite views, and both have to agree and collaborate with each other to make decisions. The way this works is that no one person can veto the other. The how/best person can't just say no to anything new, and the why/potential person can't just develop ideas forever. Instead, this step will require both partners to adopt a firm problem-solv-ing approach in order to resolve the inevitable conflicts that will arise.

And it's advisable for both partners to evaluate each idea in the set independently, before discussing them. Julia Minson, Rick Larrick, and I grouped participants into pairs and then asked them to answer questions that they were highly uncertain about, such as "How many people live in the state of Pennsylvania?" Then they discussed estimates before providing their answers. We found that when discussion partners first estimated independently and then discussed their estimates together, they were more accurate than a crowd of more than fifty judges.

Andreessen Horowitz (a16z) is a top venture capital firm — so successful that competing VCs have given the firm another name: AHo. Marc Andreessen and Ben Horowitz are the two founding partners of the firm. Marc Andreessen is a big why/potential kind of thinker. In one podcast, he discusses disruptive innovation with Harvard professor Clayton Christensen. In his blog, Andreessen posts commentaries about the future of virtual reality, China, and Alpha cities. In meetings he is known to ask big questions. Of Lyft, a ride-sharing service, he says, "Don't think about how big the taxi market is. What if people no longer owned cars?" Of OfferUp he asks, "What if all this selling online — eBay and Craigslist — goes to mobile? How big could it be?"

In contrast, his partner Ben Horowitz honed his management skills at Netscape, where he was promoted to vice president and general manager. On his blog, he has written, "The Catch-22 is that if you attempt to act on those 'big things,' you will usually do big damage. In order to move big things in a positive direction, it's generally best to focus on little things." Horowitz discusses the nitty-gritty of executing new products, and how companies should be built and run.

I'm not sure that the two of them map perfectly onto a pure why/potential and how/best focus respectively, but it is clear that they have opposite yet complementary ways of seeing the world. Horowitz doesn't try to manage Andreessen in meetings, and he appreciates his big questions. Andreessen can elevate the conversation to 10,000 feet, and Horowitz can bring it back to Earth. Yet the dynamic between the two balances them from veering too far in any direction.

CONCLUSION

The traditional way to think about an inventor is to say that the person who came up with a unique idea "invented" it. Usually we think of just one individual or hero responsible for creating an invention.

I think this is a very narrow way to define invention. Name any inventor you admire. If a decision maker somewhere didn't say yes to that person's idea, you would have never heard that inventor's name. Decision makers invent by embracing the ideas others produce. This means that decision makers — the gatekeepers of our organizations — are every bit as responsible for the creative invention as those who generated it in the first place. By reframing your role of gatekeeper into the role of inventor, you are one step closer to making creative change.

But if you truly *desire* self-disruption, as opposed to just saying you want it, be prepared to feel a bit uncomfortable. The more uncomfortable you feel, the closer you are to disrupting your traditional way of thinking. Managing your anxiety by accepting what you cannot know and going with your gut feelings is one way to do this. The second way is to use what you know to *solve* problems instead of finding them. If you frame your role as an inventor who is leading the creative process, and not as a leader who seemingly already knows the answers, you will have a better shot at embracing the creative ideas you want and improving them in the process.

5

Overcome Others' Bias against Creativity

WHEN SHAWN DAVIS'S ORIGINAL SHRIMP BURGER was featured on *Shark Tank,* Davis followed a recommendation made by many idea-selling gurus — *be prepared.* Davis (aka Chef Big Shake) knew his numbers cold. Idea-selling gurus also recommend connecting your ideas to familiar ideas that are already successful, to show that your ideas have value. Shawn Davis followed this advice, framing his burger company as another kind of turkey burger, which he described as a billion-dollar business.

Did these strategies work?

No.

Later, all the sharks passed on the concept, with one of them calling Shawn's business "risky." Another shark said, "I don't know anything about it" and "I don't like shrimp." Unfortunately for the sharks, their decision to pass cost them dearly. The revenues for Shawn's company, CBS Foods, skyrocketed from $30,000 to $5 million — in just one year. When asked later, Mark Cuban, one of the sharks, said that passing on Chef Big Shake was one of the biggest missed opportunities he had seen on *Shark Tank.*

So what's the problem? What were the idea-selling gurus missing?

Shawn Davis compared his Original Shrimp Burger to a familiar product, the turkey burger, the status quo alternative to the beef burger. Decades of research shows that people prefer the status quo to the new. The reason isn't complicated or deep. It's what people in my field call a *heuristic* — a simple truism. Status quo equals good, less uncertain, survival of the fittest, and so forth. That's it. So the advice to compare your creative idea to something familiar that is also successful could — if you don't know what you're doing — evoke the status quo bias (people's preference for ideas that exist and are familiar) and cause people to like your new idea less.

When it comes to convincing people to adopt something they haven't tried before, there is one influence strategy to rule them all. Very simply, it's to tell someone that the new idea or product *is* the status quo. Aside from simply stating that as a fact, how exactly can you convince someone that a new product is the status quo? You can accomplish this task in three different ways:

- Expose them to the product repeatedly to make it familiar to them (repeated advertising).
- Tell them that the product currently exists — the longer it has existed, the better.
- Tell them that lots of other people, respected individuals or groups, are currently using the product, demonstrating that the risks are low.

These three things — *familiarity, existence,* and *low risk* — make people feel less uncertain, and feeling certain a new product will work is what people want.

So, here then is the problem: First, creative ideas are by their very nature likely to be unfamiliar to most individuals. And if someone feels uneasy about how the product or ideas work, repeated exposure could actually confuse them more. Second, the creative idea hasn't actually existed before, let alone for a long time. And third, the creative idea is too new to have wide adoption. So, given that appealing to the status quo is one of the most powerful persuasion tactics that exists, how can we overcome the fact that our creative ideas are non-status-quo?

One thing is for sure — comparing a new idea to the status quo could simply highlight that the status quo product (in this case, the turkey burger) is low risk and good relative to your new product (the shrimp burger). After all, survival of the fittest, right? Research shows that this kind of direct comparison makes people like the status quo more than the new.

Further, merely telling people *not* to use a status quo idea, product, or process might backfire. Robert Cialdini and his colleagues conducted an experiment where they planted signs along a trail in Petrified Forest National Park in Arizona with the aim of reducing theft of petrified wood, which amounted to an average of a ton a month. The signs had different messages on them — some were positively worded and some negatively worded. The sign that said PLEASE DON'T REMOVE THE PETRIFIED WOOD IN THE PARK diminished theft the most. But the sign that said MANY PAST VISITORS HAVE REMOVED THE PETRIFIED WOOD FROM THE PARK, CHANGING THE STATE OF THE PETRIFIED FOREST contributed to the *highest* amount of theft. This latter sign reinforced the status quo. When the average person read this sign, they thought, *If everyone is taking it, well, maybe I should too.*

In other words, you can't attack the status quo bias head on by telling people not to do something many others are doing. Even if you prepare a lot, have data and a great story, it still might not protect you from the status quo bias if your ideas are creative. The reason is that your data might simply highlight that existing products or ideas are more desirable because they've been around a long time, and lots of people use them.

If rational persuasion tactics can backfire, what can you do? Since people often reject creative ideas because of the way they make them feel, why not be more proactive about managing these uncertain feelings up front?

There are three basic levers you can use to help promote feelings of interest versus anxiety in others. I have an acronym to describe the three levers: FAB.

In FAB — which stands for *fit, aha,* and *broaden* — when a person feels the fit, has an aha moment, and broadens her thinking, it is more likely she will feel hopeful, interested, and even joyful about your idea, as opposed to frustrated, bored, or anxious.

FEEL THE FIT

Simon Sinek has a popular TED talk where he asserts that the reason why Apple was so successful is that they started with why, then described how, and finally what. "If Apple were like everyone else," he says, "a marketing message from them might say, 'We make great computers. They're beautifully designed, simple to use, and user-friendly. Want to buy one?'" He then notes that this kind of marketing, while typical, usually falls flat with consumers.

Sinek then goes on to describe how Apple *actually* communicates its marketing messages. The company clearly asserts that, as he puts it, "Everything we do, we believe in challenging the status quo. We believe in thinking differently. The way we challenge the status quo is by making our products beautifully designed, simple to use, and user-friendly. We just happen to make great computers.

Want to buy one?" He then notes that people love the *why* — and this explains Apple's success.

Let me ask you a question: do you believe IBM could use the exact same strategy Apple used? Before you answer, I'd like you to do a quick thought experiment. What images do you have of IBM? Probably not images you associate with creativity — like crazy hair and hoodies. Images of corporate America and big business, perhaps? When shown the IBM logo, participants in a study exhibited less creativity than when shown an Apple logo. Evidence suggests that people think IBM is definitely not creative.

So back to the question: if IBM had stated this exact why (e.g., "Everything we do, we believe in changing the status quo ..."), would that work to sell their products? Actually, they have already tried this very strategy. Most recently they convinced the musician Bob Dylan — one of the biggest rebels of his day — to appear in a commercial for their supercomputer named Watson. So having Bob Dylan interact with Watson about love and music should evoke a big why around breaking the status quo, beauty, truth, and love, right?

Well, not exactly. The commercial was described as bizarre and creepy by one journalist. In October 2015, IBM's stock was plummeting, and it continued to decline for months after the commercial aired. Why can't IBM do what Apple did?

The simple reason is fit — or, in the case of IBM and Bob Dylan, a lack of it. Think different, consider beauty, break the status quo by making computers easy to use, dress the part (in mock turtlenecks like those worn by actors in *Star Trek* and musicians like Justin Timberlake) — all these things fit perfectly with our beliefs about creativity. So I believe Simon Sinek is overstating the value of merely having a why and missing the point of his own very good example. The why helped Apple succeed, but only because it fit with all the other cues Apple was using to sell its products. When multiple cues fit our beliefs about creativity, we like the creative idea more. We feel safe, so we don't look for flaws.

When cues are a mismatch (some fit, some don't) you begin to feel unsafe, and products seem bizarre and creepy. IBM can't make us feel safe by playing the non-status-quo card because this trait doesn't fit the IBM brand. When we don't feel the fit, we feel unsafe, and we start looking for the flaws. So while it's great to have a big why, it might not help you sell your product if all the other details just don't fit with it.

This could also mean that, assuming Apple keeps its creativity branding, it will always be harder for IBM to sell a product that consumers view as creative relative to Apple. Creative products don't fit with the IBM brand; efficient and proven products might fit better. But this could also mean something ironic for Apple. Apple may have a harder time marketing their products as non-status-quo — precisely because those kinds of products are a misfit with the Apple brand of breaking new ground.

Consider the Apple Watch, which has performed short of expectations. The Apple Watch was advertised as the first "mass-market wearable." I believe that one reason for this product's underperformance could be that Apple tried to sell it using a term that killed the feeling of fit for consumers who associated Apple solely with creativity and individuality. Saying that something is for a mass market is not inherently bad from a marketing perspective; it's only bad when it presents a mis-fit with your brand around being different and unique.

TABLE 1: CUES PEOPLE ASSOCIATE WITH CREATIVITY

TYPE OF CUE	DESCRIPTION OF CUE	EXAMPLE
Paradigm Shift	A significant change in thinking that a product or process represents.	Apple: Think Different.
Breakthrough	Doing something others failed to accomplish or did not think could be done.	Google: Larry and Sergey's mission to organize a seemingly infinite amount of information on the web.
Potential	Future possibilities opened up as a result of the product or process.	Accenture: "When technology unlocks potential, brilliant ideas come to life." Print ad, *Fortune,* October 1, 2015.
Rare	The unusualness of a product or process	National Geographic: Unique Lodges of the World, www.nationalgeographiclodges.com.
Repurposing	Taking something from one context and adapting it to a second context.	Procter and Gamble: ZzzQuil was pitched as "NyQuil without the cold medicine."
Surprise	The affective reaction—amazement, astonishment.	2014 Buick: "Hmm—take a fresh look at a Buick, it just might surprise you." Commercial, www.youtube.com/watch?v=xRk256k4pic.
Artistic	The aesthetics of the product or process.	Beautifully designed Apple products being sold in beautifully designed Apple stores.
Combination	Integrating functions, features, or other aspects that are typically distinct.	*Alien* was pitched as "*Jaws* in space."
High Tech	Concerned with the role of technology.	Chromat Aeros Sports Bra: "A high-tech undergarment that walked the runway at New York Fashion Week"—review, *Fortune* magazine, October 1, 2015.
Joy	Happiness or fun involved in engaging with something.	IKEA: The Wonderful Everyday.

Jeff Loewenstein and I published a study in which we outline the very cues you can use to communicate that your product is creative. Table 1 shows all the cues. We found that the more cues you use, the more creative people will think your product is. But remember that to provide consumers with the lovely feeling of fit when selling a creative idea, you need to make sure all your cues are in alignment. You need to make sure the branding of your company fits, the person (e.g., the CEO, celebrity, or pitch person) with whom you are associating the idea fits, and the attributes of the product all fit how we define creativity (assuming you are selling a creative product). Emphasizing that your product is for the masses — because it is a big brand, fashionable, or socially acceptable — and therefore not distinct, can ruin the feeling of fit Americans have when evaluating a creative idea.

That said, my colleagues and I have evidence that your average how/best manager holds a very different definition of creativity relative to the average American consumer. Managers believe ideas are creative if they are for the masses (e.g., big brand, socially acceptable, widely used). Managers also expect creative ideas to be highly feasible.

I realize this perspective is the opposite of what consumers believe, and possibly the opposite of what you believe. When creating a feeling of fit for your audience, though, *their* definition of creativity is important, not yours. If your definition is different than theirs, it might harm your ability to sell to them. So when selling to a manager, you could emphasize cues in Table 1. Managers do like these cues. But you also need to make sure that the cues from Table 1 that you're employing don't conflict with or detract from your ability to show that your idea is feasible and wildly appealing to the masses. The good news for you is that providing evidence that your idea garnered investor interest or many Facebook likes can *increase* the extent to which how/best managers view your idea as creative.

In other words, fit is about making sure the way you present your idea conforms with what your audience defines as creative. Different cultures may have different definitions of creativity. For example, the Chinese define creativity similarly to the way managers do. If you are selling ideas in cultures other than your own, you may want to understand more about what people in those cultures view as a fit with creativity, and what they don't, before you start selling those ideas.

Fit is not only about the characteristics of an idea. Fit can involve the characteristics of a person too. Walter Isaacson's biography of Einstein asks a quirky question: if Einstein "did not have that electrified halo of hair and those piercing eyes, would he still have become science's preeminent poster boy?" Isaacson says of course he would have. But would he? There have been many tremendous scientists who developed breakthroughs that were arguably as great as, if not greater than, Einstein's. But I bet you that the average person wouldn't be able to name them if you showed him a picture. And I also bet that the average person would recognize Einstein. Not only that, college kids still have posters of Einstein on their dorm-room walls. What could explain our continued love and adoration of Einstein, while other scientists have made no impression at all?

My colleagues Jack Goncalo and Priya Kannan-Narasimhan (at the University of San Diego) and I wanted to test what we called the "crazy-hair hypothesis." Our idea was that incidental features, like a person's hairstyle, can influence whether others like their creative ideas. We used an app that allowed us to change hairstyles on the same picture — giving a man crazy hair, like Vince Vaughn's in the movie *Swingers,* or traditional hair. We told participants a backstory, asking them to imagine they were executives at a large airline who were approached by a coworker with an idea. We then assigned who would see the crazy or traditional hair picture alongside either a practical (i.e., in-flight meals) or a creative (i.e., in-flight gambling) idea. What we found was that people liked the fit! They liked the gambling idea more when pitched by the crazy-haired executive, and they liked the meals idea more when pitched by the conventional-haired executive. But when the crazy-haired executive pitched the meals idea, they liked the idea less. And when the conventional-haired executive pitched the gambling idea, participants liked that idea less.

I suspect that one of the reasons why we revere Einstein is that all his traits fit beautifully with our beliefs about what qualities help people generate creative ideas; namely, he was a rebel and an outsider. Einstein struggled with conventional education his entire life. He wasn't able to get a conventional academic job after earning his PhD. He wrote his first breakthrough paper while sitting at a desk job in a government patent office. But he also had qualities that were unrelated to his ability to produce creative works. He had the *look* of someone creative. I propose that when it comes to successfully pitching a creative idea, the way a person looks can matter every bit as much as the branding of the company or creativity of the product. We don't want boring people selling us creative ideas. We eagerly want the feeling of fit.

Incidental features like a person's hair can influence whether we feel the fit and like their creative ideas. But I'll issue a word of warning when it comes to unconventional physical appearance. When my colleagues and I were pilot testing all the different kinds of hair, it was really difficult to find unconventional hair that was also seen as attractive. In general, people thought that big, colorful, or outlandish hair made people look less attractive. For both men and women, we found that quirky hair helped others like their creative ideas only if the quirky hair didn't make the person seem less attractive relative to conventional hair. When you are trying to make your appearance creative, you shouldn't try to do something completely bizarre. I recall hearing about an entrepreneur dressing as a banana for a pitch — which the VCs felt killed her credibility. When you are making your appearance creative, you aren't going from 0 to 1. You are going from 0 (a person in a business suit) to a different kind of 0 (a businessperson in a black turtleneck). So to make your creative image work for you, you need to have a quirky appearance that looks every bit as attractive as your conventional one.

In sum, the triumvirate of fit is making sure your company brand, product, and personal image all fit your target audience's beliefs about what indicates creativity. Mis-fits can kill the consumer's, decision maker's, or coworker's receptiveness to a creative idea.

AHA STRATEGIES

One United Artists executive rejected the movie *Star Wars* because he compared it to a childish Disney cartoon that didn't excite the imagination. The executive noted that, unlike *2001: A Space Odyssey*, a financial success, *Star Wars* has no philosophical message or angst.

You might read this and smugly think, *What an idiotic decision.* You might also feel confused as to why the executive would compare *Star Wars* to a movie like *2001.* They are both sci-fi, but otherwise not even in the same ballpark. So you could chalk up this decision to a how/best knee-jerk reaction to reject a creative idea.

The executive at United Artists also noted that *Star Wars* failed to stimulate the imagination. This evaluation should not be at all surprising, since you read in Chapter 3 about how decision makers recognize creative ideas. To an individual in a decision-making role and with a how/best focus, expensive, costly, and risky ideas conflict with self-interests like making money and protecting a personal reputation. So it makes sense that the executive said that *Star Wars* was not creative — it offers a good reason why someone who supposedly cares about and is an expert in evaluating creativity might reject an idea even if everyone else on the planet thinks the idea is hugely creative.

But there is another way to think about this reaction to *Star Wars,* one we can learn from when trying to make creative change. Is it possible that part of the reason the executive evaluated *Star Wars* in this way was not only because of poor decision making, but also because of how *Star Wars* was packaged and pitched? Was this rejection partially a function of a flubbed selling attempt?

By all accounts, when *Star Wars* was being sold by Lucas's then-agent Jeff Berg and attorney Tom Pollack, neither understood what the story was about. That might not have been their fault, because all Lucas gave them about the film was thirteen brief, handwritten pages. Furthermore, when pitching the story, they labeled it as a "big sci-fi/space adventure/Flash Gordon thing."

If you are reading this account with a how/best mindset, you might immediately think, *Aha! Lucas should have had a detailed outline, with some visual overview like a graphic novel or storyboard. His lawyer and agent should have estimated the market size for similar kinds of movies to show the potential of the film.* But in truth, I don't think either of those actions would have helped that much. Storyboards and projections do help sell ideas — especially incremental ideas (like movie sequels) — as these kinds of pitching techniques fit nicely with a how/best way of viewing the world, because they immerse people in the details. But creative ideas are different kinds of animals and so require different care and feeding to help them survive and thrive.

Before the storyboards, scripts, projections, and lattes, I think there is a critical first step when selling creative ideas. This first step is especially important when selling to a person with a strong how/best mindset. If Lucas had taken this first step, I bet that *Star Wars* could have been sold in as few as four words. Actually, I take that back. I think *Star Wars* could have been sold in two. Let me first explain why.

The United Artists executive compared *Star Wars* to a Disney cartoon, and surprisingly, *2001*. Why?

As we know from Chapter 3, when we evaluate an idea for creativity, we want to fit that idea into a box. When we choose comparison points, we usually look for those that are most ideal or representative of the box or category in our minds. For example, we have a box in our brains that tells us what a sci-fi movie looks like. If you were a movie exec in the early 1970s, *2001* was the example you would have wanted to emulate because it was the most financially successful sci-fi movie of its day. Second, we also have a box in our brains that tells us what a creative idea looks like (e.g., different, breakthrough, paradigm shift, profitable).

When you compare a new movie like *Star Wars* to an existing and successful movie in the same general category, like *2001,* the similarities look striking (e.g., both have spaceships, both have artificial intelligence), and so signal that the new movie, *Star Wars,* isn't really that new or different (or creative). For this reason, if *you* made this kind of comparison, *Star Wars* probably wouldn't fit into the creativity box in *your* brain either.

That said, the comparison between *Star Wars* and *2001* makes their differences seem quite striking — and not so favorable for *Star Wars.* You might assume that the reason *2001* was great was because it evoked deep philosophical questioning in the movie-goer. Then you might also reasonably conclude that sci-fi movies need some deep philosophical message to appeal to moviegoers and sell tickets. Obviously, *Star Wars* didn't have that kind of angst and maturity — it was, in essence, an old Western cowboys-and-Indians plot transplanted to a different galaxy, far, far away.

Now that same UA executive is looking for another category to explain this lack of fit between *Star Wars* and *2001*. The executive also compared *Star Wars* to a Disney cartoon, which at that time was seen as something only kids would watch and therefore juvenile and less broadly appealing.

So when you just describe an idea to someone, even if you tell her why it is important, you are still relying on that other person to make the kind of comparison that will help her evaluate your idea accurately. Here is the problem: Creative ideas *redefine* something, and we know that generating a creative idea requires you to think outside the box and to shift from a familiar definition to a new definition. But because people whose job it is to recognize creative ideas tend not to think outside the box, and they choose comparisons inside the box to see if your idea fits the existing box, you are now in a bind.

To make things even worse, if you are pitching an idea you think is creative, you already see the new box the idea is sitting in and how it connects to the old box. The connection is obvious to you. In fact, it is so obvious that you might not understand why the other person doesn't see it too. What you might not realize is that it is totally natural for the other person not to see the connection. The other person just sees the same box she has always seen, and she sees that your new thing fits poorly in that box — and so it won't be that great.

Think of what it would feel like to see something that makes no sense to you and doesn't fit with anything you know or is a bad fit with something you think indicates success. Better yet, play the tapping game. This game was described in the wonderful book *Made to Stick,* by Chip and Dan Heath. The game goes like this: Find a partner and sit at a table facing each other. Think of a song. Instead of singing the song, tap the song on the table for a few seconds and see if your partner can guess what it is. Can you hear the music? Of course you can — loud and clear. Now ask your partner if he can hear the music and guess what song it is. Then you can switch and see if you can guess the song your partner is tapping.

Most of the time, when I've seen people play this game, the person listening can't guess the song. This is what often happens when we pitch creative ideas. We hear fabulous music — in our own minds. We see the connections between things that seem quite different and even opposite. But the other person just hears thuds.

Matt Cronin and Jeff Loewenstein's book, *The Craft of Creativity,* describes how people produce creative ideas. They outline many terrific strategies, but three stand out for me as being especially relevant to creative change. Specifically, they describe how analogies, combination, and re-categorizations help people have an aha moment or an insight. I believe you can also use these three aha strategies to reverse-engineer insight in your listener. That is, you can engineer a kind of creative insight similar to what someone feels when they generate an idea in the first place. But you do this with the aim of pitching the idea to make someone else like and want to embrace it.

Aha Strategies: Analogy

So how could George Lucas and his team have helped executives at United Artists "hear the music" in four words or less? By using what I will call an *aha strategy.* Aha strategies are designed to help other people see connections between two things that would otherwise seem odd to combine or associate. An aha idea-pitching strategy aims to quickly and deftly make the distinctive usefulness of the new thing apparent. In other words, rather than allowing a decision maker to choose what comparison to make and running the risk that your idea will seem too similar or a poor fit to the comparison, you can use an aha strategy to provide the kind of comparison that will help them understand why the idea makes sense for them to endorse.

One powerful aha strategy is *analogy.* An analogy compares one thing to another (e.g., the circulatory system in a body is like the plumbing in a house). Analogies broaden our thinking without weighing our brains down with all the small details. Analogies can convey a new concept's likely success, feel, how it works, and what it is used for, quickly and efficiently.

Not all analogies are good for making creative change, however. Analogies are less useful for creative change if they are made within the same category (e.g., *Star Wars* is like *2001*). At best, making an analogy between your creative idea and an existing one in the same general category will make your idea seem common or just a poor fit for that category. At worst, this kind of analogy can evoke the status quo bias.

A good way to know if your analogy will help sell your idea is to think through whether it helps explain why your idea will help the person you want to convince to achieve his goals. In the movie business, executives have goals around making money, right?

If I were to pitch *Star Wars,* I would look to other movies of the day that were extremely successful financially, but in a totally different category. In the late 1960s there were categories of movies with a hero's journey, rebels, battles, and strong heroines that were not sci-fi movies. Westerns such as *The Good, the Bad, and the Ugly* and *Once Upon a Time in the West* had this flavor.

So, if it were me pitching *Star Wars* back in the day, I would have pitched it as "*High Noon* in space." *High Noon* was one of the most successful Westerns of the 1950s, so making this comparison evokes dollar signs without having to say anything about money. Showing the connection between *Star Wars* and a Western like *High Noon* also allows a person to immediately see the similarities between totally different things. Immediately, the *Millennium Falcon* is understood as the cowboy's beloved steed, the blaster is a six-shooter, and battles in space are showdowns in the town square. When we see similarities between things that are very different, this matches all the cues in our brains that tell us when something is creative (e.g., paradigm shift, rare, repurposing — all the cues in Table 1). The fact that we can visualize these similarities also allows us to see the potential future success of the idea.

Analogies are especially powerful because they allow the listener to have the same kind of aha moment that the person who generated the idea had when she first came up with it. When I give talks, I show descriptions of ideas that our subjects have rated as highly creative. One idea was a running shoe that used nanotechnology to change the thickness of the shoe's fabric to reduce blisters and cool the foot. When I show people ideas like this one, they tend to laugh. When I ask why, people give some pretty interesting responses, including "It was fun to think of something I have never thought of before," or "I just liked it," or even "It seemed odd, but I get why it would make sense."

Recognizing a creative idea can be truly joyful. Jeff Loewenstein and I found that people associated creative ideas with feelings of joy and surprise. In fact, Teresa Amabile, Sigal Barsade, Barry Staw, and I wrote a paper about the positive affect and creativity link. One finding I've always loved but that often goes unnoticed in this paper is that people tend to experience joy *after* they have a creative insight.

By using the aha strategy like an analogy, you make it easier for the listener to have the same positive reaction you did when you first generated the creative idea. This positive reaction is the feeling we get when all the pieces of a puzzle suddenly snap together and make sense. Analogies provide others with the framework that serves to organize all the copious details in such a way that your idea suddenly and obviously fits into the creative-idea box in their minds.

This explains why people often describe a creative idea as being so simple it was obvious *after the fact.* The person who saw the simplicity probably also had an analogy in mind that helped him make sense of the idea in an instant. This also means that one person can view an idea and find it beautifully simple and obvious, while another can view the same idea and see it as common and cumbersome. The first person is seeing connections to the idea with something else in a totally different category, while the second person is stuck in the same box and can't help but notice that the creative idea is a poor fit with other examples in that box.

Consider Rent the Runway, a company where, for $49 a month, subscribers can select three designer handbags, sunglasses, or dresses to rent via an online portal with shipping and insurance included. When I explain this basic information to you, you might immediately think that this idea seems pretty vanilla. Clothing rental shops are fairly common and have been around for decades. Not only that, but the typical clothing rental shop has a physical location where you can go and try on clothes. You might rightfully wonder how an online system could ensure that the clothes sent to the customer actually fit. Every person interested in fashion knows that high-fashion clothes are tricky to fit into because the sizing is so different from normal clothes.

But what if I instead gave you an analogy for this business — "the Netflix of fashion." The analogy might help you understand many aspects of the business model without getting you bogged down in the details. Because the original Netflix model — subscribing to receive movies in the mail, having a list of movies you want to see, and sending one back to receive the next — is so familiar to consumers, it immediately made the value of Rent the Runway apparent. After Rent the Runway adopted this analogy, orders jumped 122 percent between 2013 and 2014. The analogy allowed consumers to have the aha moment that the entrepreneurs themselves had when they thought up the Rent the Runway business.

Aha Strategies: Combination

Combination is another useful aha strategy. By using a combination, George Lucas would have had the option to sell *Star Wars* using just two words: *space Western*. As noted in Table 1, a combination is one cue people use to determine whether something is creative. Like analogies, combinations serve to give your listener a comparison point. But instead of noting that one thing is like the other — like an analogy — combinations serve to emphasize the new element that is created by combining two things that are usually not seen together.

Like analogies, combinations give the listener a creative experience by providing him with the building blocks to quickly and efficiently understand the distinctive use for a given idea. When we quickly understand something and see connections between things that were not apparent before, this can feel like an aha or insight to the listener.

Remember the story of Steve Sasson, the Kodak engineer who invented the digital camera in the early 1970s? This story is so famous in part because of its extreme irony. Executives at Kodak failed to adopt digital technology even though it was invented at

Kodak — a decision that is believed to have directly led to Kodak's bankruptcy in 2009.

You might think this is an example of a bias against creativity. I did too. But when I read the details of how digital technology was first pitched to Kodak's executives, I realized there was another possible explanation for Kodak's odd decision to table that very creative idea.

When Steve Sasson attempted to sell the idea for the first digital camera to executives back in the early 1970s, he used a combination aha strategy to describe it. He told executives to "think of it as an HP calculator with a lens."

Would this combination sell you?

For me a Hewlett-Packard calculator evoked the image of something complicated and cumbersome, and it had nothing to do with recording memories and more to do with recording data. But, of course, this is probably because I'm not an engineer. Perhaps, if I were an engineer, I would have liked this combination. An engineer would probably understand the kind of technology used to make powerful HP calculators and see how they might be combined with a lens to make a totally revolutionary new camera. In other words, the analogy of a calculator with a lens can tell you how the technology works, but it tells you less about the problem it helps consumers or executives solve.

Executives wondered why anyone would ever want to look at their photos on a television set. This was because Steve Sasson's first demonstration of the digital camera was to take a picture of all the executives in the conference room who sat waiting to see the technology in action. It took only a fraction of a second to capture the image, but it took over twenty seconds to transfer the image onto a cassette tape, and another thirty seconds to load up the low-quality (100 pixel x 100 pixel) black-and-white image on a television set. When the executives saw their faces emerge on the

TV screen, they were interested, but still unclear about why a consumer would care. Given this tepid reception, it makes sense that Kodak would later decide not to "cannibalize" its market share by creating a product that would compete with film.

Sasson was a brilliant engineer, and chances are that if he had pitched to other engineers, he might have succeeded. The problem was that this combination did not appeal to the goals held by executives, who really didn't care about how the idea worked. The executives themselves wanted to know why the product was distinctly useful — why consumers would want to buy it, and so what competitive advantage Kodak might derive from pursuing it.

Was there a distinct use already in the minds of consumers or a perceived competitive advantage already in the minds of executives that Sasson could have employed in the course of designing an effective combination strategy to pitch his idea? I think so. One of Kodak's biggest competitors at the time was Polaroid, developer of the first "instant" camera. As kids, we used to take what we called *Polaroids* (not *Kodaks,* even though Kodak had a competing product), using a camera that immediately spit out a physical photo that would develop in front of our eyes. So, one distinct use that was already in the minds of consumers (and Kodak executives) back then was the notion of an instant camera.

Second, if you were to see your picture on TV in the 1970s, back when only stars of TV and movies were on TV, how would that make you feel? Like a movie star, perhaps? Imagine the reception from Kodak executives if Sasson had shown them his invention, put their picture on the TV screen, and told them they were "instant movie stars."

Who knows if this combination, "instant movie star," would have been enough to overcome the how/best focus Kodak had adopted as best practice in the 1970s. The point is that we cannot discount the way the digital camera was sold to executives as contributing to why this technology that could have saved the company was rejected outright.

When designing a combination (or analogy) to sell a creative idea, you need to think very carefully about the goals of your audience. If your audience consists of other engineers or designers who care about how things work, then using a combination that helps them understand the inner workings of an idea can work beautifully to sell that idea. However, if your audience consists of consumers or end users, they probably couldn't care less about how the idea works — and, in fact, they may not even want to know how it works. What end users might want to know is how the idea would solve their distinct and unique problems.

Consider the combination "toilet to tap." It was used by the government to try and sell treatment plants that convert wastewater into drinking water. This is actually a great idea that is very creative and helps solve an incredibly important problem related to the drought in California.

"Toilet to tap" has an alliterative ring to it, for sure, and to an engineer — or to a person who cares about how a problem is solved — it can seem like a clever, nonobvious combination. For that matter, to a politician, it might scream *economical*. And in fact, "toilet to tap" water is half the cost of desalinated water and less costly than imported water. So using the combination of "toilet to tap" would have been pretty effective in selling this solution and pushing it internally through the engineering and political ranks.

But to an end user like you and me, this "toilet to tap" combination has an extreme gross-out factor. When you read newspaper articles that talk about controversial "toilet to tap" initiatives, scientists who describe the problem will go into even grosser detail, like "It has no taste," and "It is processed a lot." Ick! It is very difficult to see how the "toilet to tap" combination solves the problems consumers have with it. It's like trying to sell a nightclub as "vomit free," adding, "It doesn't smell anymore!" and "We had to work really hard to clean it up."

So what do you do when your idea involves something that is socially unacceptable — like wastewater? A combination contains a piece of the prior thing, in this case something that was seen as distasteful — but combinations can also serve to transform something distasteful into something good.

Consider AOBiome, an MIT startup where one top manager hasn't showered in thirteen years. AOBiome believes bathing is a bad thing because it destroys the natural bacteria on your skin that protects you from all kinds of diseases, acne, eczema, and more. AOBiome's flagship product, AO+ Mist, introduces *N. eutropha* — an ammonia-oxidizing bacteria — that's applied to the skin. Imagine trying to sell this product by describing it, and then telling a customer to spray it on her face, pitching it as "odorless." Yuck!

A *New York Times Magazine* journalist profiled AO+ in an article titled "My No-Soap, No-Shampoo, Bacteria-Rich Hygiene Experiment." The article went viral in May 2014 and launched AO+ into the public eye by holding the most-emailed slot for a month. After the article launched, the startup received over twenty thousand emails in two weeks requesting the product. What this article title did was to combine two things that were seen to be opposite: bacteria and hygiene. This combination was not only surprising because it linked the unexpected; it also transformed something gross (bacteria) into something opposite and good (hygiene).

A recent study by Jonah Berger and Katie Milkman at the Wharton School examined which *New York Times* articles made the most-emailed list. They found that people wanted to share stories that had practical value, but every bit as important — if not more important — was whether the article made people feel *in-*

terested and *surprised*: the two feelings most likely to result when people have an aha experience.

AOBiome and the "toilet to tap" initiative are both great ideas that solve important problems, but only AOBiome's product was widely adopted. Remember that for aha strategies to work, you have to emphasize how a solution solves a problem that your audience has. Sometimes you can combine opposites and attract attention in a positive way, as in the case of AOBiome. But other times, as in the case of "toilet to tap," you are unlikely to combine anything with *toilet* that consumers want to drink. In this case, a combination strategy might not work, and an analogy might not take you far enough away from your starting point. If you are in this boat, there is another strategy you might consider: re-categorization. You can re-categorize your idea (e.g., "toilet to tap") into something else that people actually want (e.g., clean water).

Aha Strategy: Re-categorization

Sometimes we need to transform how people are thinking about a given idea to show that ideas that don't initially fit with our beliefs about how the world works actually fit beautifully. Consider the case of active-duty commander Brian Delaney, a U.S. Navy officer who is paralyzed. Take a moment for that statement to sink in. The navy has a general policy to medically retire people who cannot walk. So why would the navy agree to keep Brian Delaney on active duty — and as a commander, no less?

On October 30, 2013, Commander Delaney was heading home on his motorcycle after a long day's work aboard his ship, USS *Harpers Ferry*. He took a turn too fast and hit a guardrail, severing his spinal cord. When it became clear that Commander Delaney would not walk again, the Navy Medical Board concluded that he should be medically retired.

While this decision was expected, Commander Delaney still felt like he had something to contribute and wanted to continue to serve. A very senior navy leader in San Diego agreed that Delaney was able to continue working in a support role and lobbied Navy Personnel Command to let him. When asked how he got them to allow Delaney to continue serving, he said it was because of Delaney's excellent prior record and competence. But when pushed to describe the actual strategy he used, he said, "When I think about leadership, I don't think about the physicality of a leader. I think about his characteristics — integrity, stamina, charisma — all the person's attributes. Here was a guy at death's door, in an incredible amount of pain, but talk about toughness and perseverance and the will to live ... he flatlined three times!" What this navy leader did was to re-categorize Delaney's weakness and paralysis into a leadership strength — the physical and mental toughness to persevere.

People make decisions and evaluations by placing things into boxes or categories. Categorizations help us to efficiently navigate the world. In Chapter 2, we looked at our implicit beliefs, which tend to be organized by category. For example, people have implicit beliefs (i.e., stereotypes) that leaders are strong and charismatic. So when we see someone exhibiting a trait that indicates weakness, this presents a poor fit with the category of leader, and so we categorize this person as a nonleader.

But what this navy officer did was to redefine and expand the definition of strength to include mental toughness and the will to live. By broadening the definition of strength in a way that was consistent with Delaney's traits, he made it easy to re-categorize Delaney's perceived weakness as a strength. In fact, the officer cleverly made Delaney's struggle a *reason* to make him a leader.

Consider maternal-leave policies — policies that allow women some period of time at home after the birth of a child. Framing this policy as a "maternal leave" reinforced the stereotype that women should be categorized as belonging in the home, not at work. Instead, men were the ones who belonged at work. Case in point: there was no paternity leave or, if there was, it was very short in duration, to the point of being more like a personal day.

For this reason, many women decided to decline taking maternal leave to avoid the stigma of being seen as more focused on home life than work life. For example, prior to 2005, less than 3 percent of female faculty at Princeton University took maternal leave, but this number increased dramatically when maternal leave was reframed as "parental leave" and extended to both mothers and fathers. By re-categorizing maternal leave as parental leave, you expand the definition of home life to include men as well as women. This effectively reduced the stigma for women who wanted to be seen as committed to their jobs.

Creative Storytelling with Aha Strategies

We know from books like *Made to Stick* by Chip and Dan Heath that telling emotional stories is important for helping people remember and use our ideas. When it comes to creative ideas, though, the stories we tell need to be altered a bit to accommodate the fact that these kinds of ideas don't always fit with what your listener knows and expects.

If you just tell the story and show people the numbers, you risk the likelihood that the other person will just hear thuds because in his mind he is comparing your idea to something that makes it seem odd and out of place. This is exactly why repeated advertisements can fail when the ideas they put forward are creative.

So before getting into the details of the actual story, a quick recap: Providing listeners with an analogy, re-categorization, or combination can give them a comparison point they are familiar with, but that might be significantly different from the idea you are proposing. By drawing comparisons between your ideas and other ideas in a different category, you make it more likely that listeners will have the kind of creative aha moment that results in feelings of interest, enjoyment, and surprise — the kinds of feelings that make people want to share, buy, and embrace ideas.

BROADEN

When it comes to embracing creative ideas, a broader focus can help someone feel more comfortable and hopeful about all the things that are just not yet known about a new idea. Instead of selling with the aim of showing the value of an existing idea, you can instead sell with the aim of *broadening* the other person's role from expert to inventor.

In other words, you are moving expert decision makers into an inventor role by giving them a problem to solve, or motivation to solve a problem. For one, you can get decision makers to brainstorm with you about your idea by asking for feedback. I like to call this strategy *the feedback pitch.*

Broaden Strategy: The Feedback Pitch

Did you know that people tend to like and say yes to their own creative ideas? In fact, we know that when people have creative ideas that they feel proud of, they think of them as indicating their genius, and they also rate them as more likely to succeed than other ideas. While this might not surprise you, it might intrigue you to hear that by allowing others to make small changes to your idea, you may dramatically increase the likelihood that they will also say yes to your creative solutions.

Seeking lots of feedback from many different types of people is a good strategy if you want to improve the quality of your creative ideas. Once someone gives you feedback on an idea, you have an opportunity. If you implement their feedback and let them know by thanking them, you have now increased the likelihood that they will say yes to the idea in the future. There are two reasons for this.

- First, now that they have made their change, they psychologically own part of the idea. When we feel psychological ownership of something, we want to embrace it.
- Second, when we see new ideas the first time, they can seem psychologically distant (e.g., abstract or foreign) and potentially odd, but when our own feedback is integrated into the idea, that idea suddenly seems more concrete, familiar, and safe — so we like it more.

The great news about the feedback pitch is that these changes don't necessarily need to be large to make a large impact in the other person's satisfaction with the idea. Small wording changes or changes in formatting are sometimes sufficient to make the other person feel ownership of the idea and like it more.

Another way to think about selling an idea is to turn the selling into a problem-solving session where you collaborate on how to make the idea better. Research by Kimberly Elsbach at UC Davis and Rod Kramer at Stanford examined Hollywood pitches and found that when artists pitched film ideas to producers by taking their suggestions into account and collaborating with them, producers were more likely to view the artist as having strong creative potential.

It is important to acknowledge the difference between asking for feedback and asking for help. Asking for feedback can involve your saying, "I think this idea has potential, what do you think?" Asking for help requires that you acknowledge your prior way of solving the problem has failed and you need a new paradigm to solve it. If you were asking for help, you might say, "I've tried many different ways to solve the problem and they didn't work — do you have any ideas?"

Seeking help from others can be a good strategy to improve your ability to generate creative ideas. When you ask for help, you get better information because the other person knows not to recommend a course of action you have already taken or thought about. Instead, when you ask the other person for help, she is working to suggest something new you have not yet tried. This maximizes the likelihood that you will receive a solution that is valuable because it is different from the failed paradigm you have been using — and so more likely to solve the problem.

However — and this is important — there are also huge downsides to asking for help. Dishan Kamdar and I collected data in several organizations. Help-seeking is routinely positively related to generating ideas. However, seeking help also kills the seeker's reputation. Seeking help is negatively related to whether people think you are a leader, are efficient at implementation, and are competent in general. In short, people who seek help from others might reap a huge informational gain but face a huge reputational cost. My work with Ashleigh Shelby Rosette and Dave Lebel shows that this is particularly true of male leaders — those who seek help are seen as less competent than those who don't.

Feedback-seeking is quite different from help-seeking. When you seek feedback, you aren't looking for information you have not yet considered. When you are seeking feedback, you are trying to get a sense of how the other person thinks about your idea and what improvements he would make. Seeking feedback does not involve your saying anything negative about your idea — you are simply asking, "What do you think?" And when you ask that question, you are more likely to receive information or ideas you have heard before. But that's okay. Your goal isn't necessarily to make this idea better — although that would be great if you could. Your goal is to *sell* it.

When selling an electric car, salespeople know to address range anxiety. When selling insurance, people know to anticipate questions around why premiums are so high. But when it comes to creative ideas, it is very difficult to accurately predict the concerns people might have. So rather than expend your energy trying to do something that is probably a waste of time, why not just ask them?

There are five steps to implementing a feedback pitch.

Step 1: Make a list of all the people whose approval you need in order to green-light a given idea. Don't forget cross-functional approval (e.g., legal, research and development, and any other teams that are not your own) in addition to your senior managers.

Step 2: Make a plan to approach each person one-on-one with enough lead time to allow you to meet with them as well as make any changes you've agreed upon. Depending on your company culture, you may decide to make these meetings formal or informal (e.g., in a formal meeting, at lunch, at the water cooler, or a quick chat in the hallway).

Step 3: When asking someone for her feedback, take the opportunity to turn the feedback session into a collaboration. If decision makers tell you they don't like something, don't try to defend what you did; instead, ask them what they would do to change the idea and make it better. Then have a discussion and brainstorm about whether there is a way to bring their changes more in line with your vision.

Step 4: Follow up with each person, thanking them for their feedback and showing how you implemented it. Let them know that it makes the original idea that much better (assuming you believe it).

Step 5: Ask for their approval. The point of the feedback pitch is to try to collaborate more with decision makers instead of using traditional sales approaches. In a traditional sales approach, you are trying to sell and defend what you currently have to offer. When selling a creative idea, you are selling the potential of something that might not exist yet.

You might worry and say, "I don't want decision makers taking credit for my ideas." I get this concern. But decision makers can take credit for your ideas even if you don't use a feedback pitch to tell them about it. They can brag and say, "It was my vision that allowed the idea to be funded," etc. Steve Jobs was routinely accused of stealing others' ideas. My advice is this. If the decision maker claims the idea as his, think of it this way: You won. You successfully made creative change — no small feat. That's something *you* can brag about.

By collaborating with decision makers, you are helping them overcome their status quo biases. The person whose feedback you have asked for now feels more ownership over the idea, so she's less likely to be risk averse. This person has discussed the idea with you in detail — so now the idea is more familiar to her. Last, this person has generated solutions to improve the idea with you. You have gotten her into the brainstorming paradigm — and potentially into an *inventor mindset* — which helps her think more deeply about the idea, so she is less likely to make knee-jerk how/best decisions.

Broaden Strategy: Make Them Feel the Failure

When I talk to entrepreneurs, many complain that pitching to the typical VC or angel is a waste of time. They argue that most investors are so entrenched in the how/best way of viewing the world that there is no way they can provide the kind of certainty those investors crave. They say that you have to find someone who is already in a broad *inventor* mindset if you want to get your creative idea adopted. Basically, they believe that only a small percentage of investors are open to new ideas in the first place. The challenge, in these entrepreneurs' view, is finding those people.

I agree with this advice. It is true that sometimes you cannot convince people and cannot change their minds. It is also true that some audiences are more likely to be receptive to certain ideas than others. Take early adopters. Early adopters in the technology community are those who enjoy trying new technologies before anyone else. People in this community get special social currency for being in the know about new technological advances, so companies can benefit by using early adopters as a testing ground for new products.

So one piece of advice that follows is to look for audiences or decision makers who you think might already have an inventor mindset. People with reputations for making bold and creative decisions are a good place to start.

Another piece of advice is to look for decision-makers who have expertise in a variety of different domains — not just one. Page Moreau and her colleagues found that people with expertise in film didn't like the digital camera relative to novices, but people with expertise in film *and* scanner technology did like the digital camera relative to novices. In my experience, people with expertise in two or more different disciplines tend to be more curious and interested in — and less threatened by — the new, relative to those who have deep skills in a single discipline.

That said, sometimes you are stuck having to convince a single decision maker. When you are stuck with one decision maker with a strong how/best mindset, do you have any recourse? Is this game over?

Rob B. McClary, PhD, sometimes teaches courses on creativity and innovation to officers in the U.S. Army. One day, during this course, a major told Rob, "I don't care if an idea is creative, I care if the idea works." What McClary did next was masterful. He told the major, "That is exactly how your enemy wants you to think. How do you know if an idea worked? You know because you have done it before. Your enemies want you to do what has worked in the past — because that way they can predict what you will do next and beat you. Thinking that you want what is proven — as opposed to what is new and unexpected — is the exact kind of thinking that will lose you the entire war."

Dr. McClary didn't overcome the major's objection by talking about the value of creativity and the future benefit of ideas. He overcame his objection by telling him that his current way of thinking would lead to utter failure. By saying, "That is exactly how your enemy wants you to think," he likely made the major feel slightly ashamed and fearful of being duped by the enemy. In other words, Rob McClary didn't just run through the facts — he made the major feel the failure.

Many executives I work with say they already use this technique. But when I look at what they are actually doing, most show future projections or downward trends from past to present. What they *don't* do is create a story that links the status quo directly to failure in a way that makes executives feel anxiety, shame, or even embarrassment about it.

I once worked with a company that believed that the key to winning in the marketplace was to implement "low-hanging fruit" — the most feasible and easiest product improvements. They believed that if a product is easy and cheap to make, customers will buy it because they'll see that you can offer cheaper products faster than competitors can.

So I tested their assumption. I asked decision makers in the company to rate a series of ideas they were considering implementing according to how feasible they were. I also asked a group of their customers to rate how much they wanted to buy these same ideas. What I found was a strong negative correlation between idea feasibility and how much customers wanted to buy these very same ideas. Customers didn't know if executives thought the ideas were feasible or not — they didn't care. They were bored with products the company wanted to produce. When I showed this data to the company, they promptly reorganized their decision-making structure.

After reading this book, it will come as no surprise to you to learn that Dr. Fogarty's balloon catheter paper, about a technology that is now the standard of care, was first rejected by all the major medical journals. He noted that academics on editorial boards were simply not focused on whether procedures had basic utility to the patient. It was only when Fogarty's mentor, Dr. Cranley, made a few calls that he was able to convince one editor to publish the paper. However, mere publication was not enough to spur creative change, because at first nobody used the new method — even though it was demonstrably better than the status quo.

When I asked Dr. Fogarty why physicians would not employ a method that would guarantee a better patient outcome, he told me, "Surgeons are taught to do the same thing the same way all the time." Doctors are told by the establishment (e.g., traditional hospital administrators) that if they don't do things the same way for everyone, they could get sued, and the hospital won't protect them.

Furthermore, he said that creative ideas in medicine can "put the establishment out of business. The existing physicians — who don't know how to use the new procedure — don't have the time or interest in learning it. After all, if they do learn the new technique and it catches on, then this can threaten a physician's status as being an expert and highly proficient in the old technique."

Dr. Fogarty's new method involved making a very small incision; it was relatively noninvasive. But cutting and making big incisions was part of how surgeons had defined their role for years. As he told me, "The bigger the incision, the bigger the surgeon."

Creative change did eventually happen, and surgeons adopted Dr. Fogarty's balloon catheter, but it came about in an unexpected way. A clever lawyer used Dr. Fogarty's balloon catheter paper in a case suing surgeons who had used the old procedure. The lawyer argued that the doctors were negligent because they failed to use a new procedure that would have guaranteed better patient outcomes. The lawyer won his case, and the balloon catheter became the gold standard of care — saving thousands of lives immediately after it was implemented.

The balloon embolectomy catheter remains an industry standard today. When describing this story, Dr. Fogarty noted with sincerity, "This is the only time in the history of medicine that a lawsuit helped improve patient care." I believe the lawsuit forced people to broaden their perspective by making them fear the status quo more so than Fogarty's invention.

People make creative change only when they realize their current definitions are blocking them from achieving what they want. Our current definitions have to fail in some respect. When something fails utterly, when the status quo is unacceptable, we have no choice but to broaden our thinking and move into a creative space. After all, feeling hope for the future necessarily means that you want something better than what you currently have.

Even people who are entrenched in their status quo beliefs — beliefs that have existed for a long time — can still redefine and embrace creative change. But when people hold fast to a given definition about the world, they don't change because they want to. They don't change if they know change is the right thing to do. They don't change if they know the benefits and costs of staying put. They only change if they feel something. They change when they feel embarrassed, frustrated, or ashamed of the status quo.

I believe that effectively pitching a creative idea and communicating it to good effect is every bit as complicated and difficult as generating a terrific invention. There are certainly other strategies well known in the "power and influence" literature that will also help you pitch creative ideas (e.g., build coalitions, use reciprocity, make sure people like you). But be mindful when pitching to avoid evoking the status quo bias. If you use FAB, the fit, aha, broaden framework, you are more likely *not* to evoke the status quo bias, and instead help the other person feel hope and interest for your idea.

6

Cultivating Creative Change in Your Organization

IN SEPTEMBER 2015, STEVE MOLLENKOPF — THE CEO at smartphone chip giant Qualcomm — stated, "Now we are in a position where we have to pivot the company." Qualcomm had just lost a major contract with Samsung, and a few months earlier it had announced a 15 percent cut in its global workforce. Share price had dropped precipitously. And on top of all that, the smartphone chip market was becoming more competitive. By all accounts, Qualcomm was in trouble. But when you hear executives at Qualcomm speak, they express confidence in their highly innovative culture. They say that they have to be creative or die — and they don't plan to die.

Qualcomm's situation could signal the beginning of uncreative destruction, or they could nail the decision and pivot beautifully. But, could a company's culture — even an innovative one — make it harder for people in that company to make effective decisions when creativity is involved? After all, a company can undergo uncreative destruction even if it lauds innovation and wants more of it. In other words, just wanting to pivot in the right direction isn't enough to ensure you will. So what can companies do? In my experience, there are three major organizational-level barriers to creative change. I'll describe each in turn and the resulting solutions that can help you make creative change in your organization.

PROBLEM # 1: CULTURE WITHOUT COURSE CORRECTIONS

No one could believe it when Nokia failed. Nokia invented the smartphone in 1996. It was a nimble Finnish company that started out as a wood pulp mill in 1865 with diverse interests in products such as paper, electricity, and rubber galoshes. Nokia was also able to adapt. In the early '90s, Nokia got rid of all of its businesses except telecom — a move that, for over a decade, made them the largest mobile-phone company in the world.

Nokia was lauded for its innovation prowess, and the company could seemingly do no wrong. It was spending resources to develop creative new products, but also exploiting and improving current products. By all accounts, Nokia had an innovative culture. So what then was the flaw that led to its ultimate demise? In short, it could not course correct. When the market started moving in a direction away from phone hardware and toward phone software (apps, specifically), Nokia couldn't or wouldn't shift. Could Nokia's "innovative" culture have prevented it from pivoting in a new direction?

I realize it is very trendy to talk about creative culture. You might be puzzled to know that research in this area sidesteps this issue of creative organizational culture altogether, instead talking about work environments that support creativity by providing resources, freedom, and autonomy to workers. In other words, the inference is that cultures — which have rules of behavior and assumptions — can kill creativity. The solution is to give your creative people resources and get out of their way so they can innovate.

How do you know the kind of culture you're in? You usually don't, until you break a rule. If you break a strongly held cultural rule, you will know because you will likely be punished. Bear in mind that the overall point of a culture is to establish solidarity around the rules. There is another term for a rule — status quo. Michele Gelfand, at the University of Maryland, and her colleagues note that being in a "tight" or strong culture means that if you break the rules — if you violate the status quo — you will be punished and possibly ostracized. In contrast, "loose" or weak cultures tend to be more creative because the rules are more informal and ambiguous — so people don't necessarily know when you break them.

To me, a strong culture is one of the most powerful vehicles enforcing the status quo bias. Strong cultures are the source of "not invented here" (NIH) — the belief that the status quo is the best and most appropriate process for any company to adhere to. Yes, I'm going to say it: I believe strong corporate culture is often a creativity killer.

In my experience, most companies are not built with a creative culture in mind. I've read the hype promoted by management consultants about how you can build a culture that supports creativity on top of a highly bureaucratic one. I think these kinds of management initiatives are a waste of time and money.

Strong-arming change when creativity is involved is a Sisyphean task. The more you try to force people to change closely held assumptions and definitions, the more they will do the opposite (because simply mandating that they change the status quo can still reinforce the status quo bias). So, just as I noted in the last chapter when I introduced you to FAB, the fit, aha, broaden framework, when it comes to making creative change at the organizational level, you need to attack the problem sideways. You need to somehow evoke positive feelings and curiosity about what is new — and at the very least raise concern and worry about the old.

This is not easy. Fortunately, you also have the option to build in course corrections. Trying to change a culture requires that you force people to change all their assumptions and values. But building in course corrections is a bit more focused, requiring a company to change one specific assumption or value at a time. The two strategies for course correcting that I'll propose target one specific thing holding people back, one thing keeping them from adopting the new and ultimately making creative change. In this way, you can address creative change on a case-by-case basis rather than in one big, costly move.

Course Correct: Disrupt Organizational Definitions Holding You Back

Organizational cultures reflect what companies value. And values can reinforce certain definitions. Sometimes definitions can relate to corporate strategy, such as the case of Qualcomm focusing on chips in phones. Sometimes this definition relates to a company's identity, such as Nokia's focus on engineering hardware. Sometimes definitions are assumed and potentially invisible, such as when Nitin Nohria, the dean of Harvard Business School, realized in 2013 that the HBS student body and faculty were defining women as communal but not high achieving — an implicit definition that became apparent only when he saw data that confirmed it.

The point is that cultures uphold definitions that come in many shapes and forms, and these definitions can often harm creative change. If a new discovery is seen as being inconsistent with a company's basic definition (e.g., a poor fit with strategy), that discovery will be ignored. If the market is moving in a new direction opposite from how the company is defining itself (as in the case of Nokia), the company will be stuck. If companies recognize only opportunities that fit their definitions, they are in a bind when real creativity comes along.

The sad truth is that sometimes companies need to fail utterly before they realize that their definitions are holding them back. What I find interesting is, if you ask people in the trenches which definitions are suffocating the company, they seem to know the answer. But top-level executives in large organizations often don't know what their employees know. Cutting-edge research by Cristina Gibson at the University of Western Australia and her colleagues shows that those who are closer to the top tend to be more out of touch with the feelings and perceptions of those beneath them in the organizational hierarchy.

Course Correct: Identify problematic definitions. One recommendation is to start encouraging your employees in the trenches to answer this basic question: "What definitions or assumptions are holding us back? Why?" I recommend you provide employees with an anonymous survey — ask this open-ended question, and then have someone go through and tally the responses to see which is the most common.

One company I consulted with found that the definition most nominated for holding the company back was "Fast growth is good." Their employees believed that fast growth was killing the company's ability to deliver a quality product.

I believe that gathering data systematically is key to identifying which definitions are problematic. That's because once you identify a problematic definition, you are invariably going to feel resistance to changing it. Having the actual data in hand can help you feel the failure, and broaden your thinking.

Even if you don't have the time to run a survey, you can systematically analyze employee feedback on websites like Glassdoor. Glassdoor is like a Yelp for corporations. Most restaurant owners really care about their Yelp reviews. Yet, ironically, I've never met a manager who cared about Glassdoor reviews.

I think this is a great example of a widely held definition getting in the way. Managers define Glassdoor as a tool to help employees get jobs, and where disgruntled employees go to complain. I'm suggesting that you re-categorize websites like Glassdoor as a modern version of a listening post or an exit interview where you can glean valuable employee feedback. The way you can discern between idiosyncratic complaints and real issues is to identify how often the same specific complaint is mentioned by different employees. In any case, monitoring the feedback on Glassdoor is a cheap and easy way to get back in touch with definitions that might be holding your company back.

I can already tell you one problematic definition I suspect your company has: rejected ideas are seen as bad. When I consult for clients, invariably I'll hear the stories about all the ideas that got away. One client told me that several product prototypes were sitting on her shelf gathering dust years after being rejected by the corporate steering committee. Two of those products, however, had been adopted by a competitor and became smash successes!

So one possibility is that the next big thing is already here — in your office, or in one of your colleagues' offices. Just because something was rejected once should have no bearing on whether the idea was great. You just got through reading the science revealing the bias against creativity. Like every other organization, your organization probably suffers from this. So before spending more money on R&D, go back through the file drawer of rejected ideas. Look to see what prototypes are lingering on executives' shelves. Ask executives if any rejected idea has stuck with them, or if there might be a product among them that they've been wondering about. If a product evoked enough of an emotional reaction to be remembered by a decision maker, check it out again using the self-disruption strategies in Chapter 4. You might just discover a latent gold mine. And the best part is, you won't have to increase your research and development budget to do it.

Course Correct: Use FAB for the masses to shift definitions. Once you pinpoint the definitions holding your company back, it's time to strategize about how to change them. It's important to realize that any changes your company made were probably hard for you — and as such, they are going to be very hard for employees too. Further, you don't want to make the mistake of reinforcing the status quo bias when evoking the change (as mentioned in Chapter 5). Hence, I recommend using FAB, but only on a mass scale to help people shift their definitions and to embrace the new.

The story of how Harvard Business School (HBS) decided to promote women began when it had no choice but to broaden because it felt the failure. HBS dean Nitin Nohria notes that this feeling started when a female faculty member raised her hand and asked, "What is the gender composition of the various honors that we just awarded to these students?" After the question was asked, the HBS administration looked at the data. The pattern was clear. Male and female MBA students had equal GMAT scores and grades when they were admitted to the program. But by the time they graduated, male MBA students were getting much better grades relative to female MBA students.

When they saw the data and felt the failure, Nohria noted, "I think it is important for us to better understand what is holding people back." What was holding HBS back? Well, there was the implicit definition that women at HBS were communal but not high achieving. After realizing that this definition was making it harder for HBS to authentically promise equal opportunity and recruit the best women, they came up with a plan to dismantle it. They used a version of FAB to attack this problem.

First, Nohria apologized, and did so publicly. In front of six hundred alumni he said that women at Harvard "felt disrespected, left out, and unloved by the school. I'm sorry on behalf of the business school. The school owed you better, and I promise it will be better." What is wonderful about this apology is that it doesn't talk about the status quo. He doesn't state that women are widely discriminated against at HBS (the status quo). He doesn't mandate that people no longer discriminate against women; doing so might have evoked the very status quo bias he wanted to avoid. Instead, he focuses on how women felt — the very reason why the status quo is so egregiously wrong. He helped the audience feel the failure of the status quo, and he showed that HBS felt the failure too.

That isn't all HBS did. One aha strategy you can employ to re-categorize and shift people's beliefs is to inundate them with counterexamples. In this case, the belief was "women are communal and not achievement oriented." So to counter this belief, the HBS administration told female students to raise their hands in class. They told female faculty to be tough in the classroom, not just supportive. They pledged to increase the number of case studies that focused on female protagonists by 20 percent (only 9 percent of case studies at the time were about women).

When using re-categorization you expand the existing definition to include its opposite. You expand the definition from "women are communal, *not* high achieving" to "women are communal *and* high achieving." The way to expand this definition is by giving people whose minds you want to change example after example after example. One very clear example won't work. That's because people have what is called a *confirmation bias* — they will disregard information that disconfirms stereotypical beliefs in favor of information that confirms their beliefs. The point is that using one example is a start, but it is not enough. You need to inundate people with lots of examples, and with examples they do not expect.

Consider the Post-it Note — one of the most beloved innovations of our time. Do you know how management at 3M first reacted to the Post-it? They called it "scratch paper," and noted with authority that you can give scratch paper away for free, but certainly nobody is going to buy it.

In 1978 3M marketing executives first tried to sell Post-its to consumers. The company went to four cities — Tulsa, Denver, Richmond, and Tampa — and inundated consumers with ads. The ads didn't work. Consumers didn't care. Distributors didn't care. Post-its nearly died an early death.

So how did the Post-it survive? Art Fry is often credited with inventing the Post-it. Most people who write about him focus on how he developed the idea while in choir practice when he realized he needed an adhesive bookmark he could easily remove from the pages of his hymnal book. But I think Fry's critical insight was actually in how to sell the Post-it. He didn't try to sell executives in the company outright with traditional pitches and slide presentations. He did something far simpler, and far more powerful.

Fry started by getting 3M's internal administrative staff addicted to Post-its. Even more clever, that administrative staff worked for 3M's senior managers. He didn't tell them how to use Post-its, or demonstrate the use for them, or tell them others had used them. He just gave Post-its to them and said, "Try this." One marketing director noted, "Once people started using them it was like handing them marijuana. Once you start it, you can't stop."

By addicting the administrative staff to the Post-its, Fry convinced two senior vice presidents, Geoffrey Nicholson and Joseph

Ramey, that the Post-it had promise. Even though the original Post-it market launch failed, these two senior executives got into a problem-solving (versus problem-finding) space and wanted to know *why* the product had failed. Nicholson and Ramey clearly had an inventor mindset. So they decided to gather more data. They took matters into their own hands and went door to door — giving the product away at banks and offices in Richmond, Virginia's business district. Over the course of a very short time, they watched consumers invent all sorts of uses for Post-its, and they realized that giving away Post-its for free might indeed be the best way to advertise them.

What transpired next was called the Boise Blitz. Fry and other folks at 3M handed out free samples of Post-its in Boise, Idaho. Fry noted that "10 sheet samples led to complete addiction." After Post-its were given away, a whopping 90 percent of people reordered — and paid for them.

So going back to the principles in Chapter 5, traditional advertising and exposing a person to a product over and over won't help if people don't understand the product to begin with. Sometimes, when a product is new, you need to allow people to try it. But not just consumers — your own internal people.

I'm not talking about *dogfooding* — a Silicon Valley term used to describe when a company *makes* employees use their main product. Dogfooding happens only when a company has already signed on to develop an idea. For example, when Uber first opened its doors, one of the ways it succeeded and scaled up was by having all its employees use the service, understand for themselves how it worked in the real world, and recommend it to others. I think this is a great strategy, but it's a bit different from the one I'm proposing. I'm suggesting that before you make the decision to sell a product or implement a process, you first give your employees the opportunity to experiment with it.

Allowing your employees to experiment with a product before anybody green-lights it can help them self-disrupt and see the value. When we brainstorm with a product, it automatically shifts us from a problem-finding to a problem-solving mode. The reason Art Fry said that giving people ten Post-it Note sheets would result in addiction was because ten sheets allowed people enough trials to experiment with and to find useful purposes for the product.

A lot of companies believe you need to pay focus groups to test ideas. Why? Why can't you just give the ideas to your employees for free? Let your own employees give feedback to the designers, and then start to problem solve and improve the product. Let your employees be inventors — especially if those employees are in your regulatory departments, like legal. People have fun inventing, and just because they didn't come up with the product, it doesn't mean they aren't inventing when they use it. One person's feedback can be the key insight to making the idea work.

Placing people both inside and outside your organization into an inventor's state of mind can help them overcome their how/best resistance to creative ideas and will very likely allow them to embrace those ideas.

This was the original magic of the Better Place vision. Journalists will tell you that Better Place failed because customers had to live with inconvenience and expensive cars, but they note with confusion that Better Place customers still like the concept and the product. I just visited a friend in Israel who still drives her Better Place car to work — and wishes the company had succeeded. How is this possible? Consumers are all self-interested, right? Wrong. Turns out, people want to save the world. They want to be part of a creative process to make the world a "better place." Shai Agassi put his customers in the inventor mindset by asking, "How do you do this, still within the boundary of the science we know today?" — meaning how can we use the technology we currently have to reduce dependence upon oil? If you were a Better Place customer, then you weren't an entitled consumer. You weren't just buying a car to get to work. If you were a Better Place customer, you were on the path toward invention — engaged in learning how to save Israel from dependence on oil. You were a hero.

In sum, if you want to make creative change en masse and shift from one ingrained definition to another that may seem to be in opposition to it, you first need to figure out the definitions that are holding your organization back. Then pick and choose strategies from the FAB methodology in Chapter 5 to help people change those counterproductive definitions.

PROBLEM # 2: CONFLICT WITHOUT COMMUNICATION

In Chapter 3, I described a study where my colleagues and I showed that decision-making roles shifted how people in those roles defined creativity. We have gone into a couple of organizations and replicated this finding, showing that decision makers define creativity differently than their workers do. We looked at thousands of people in the United States and China and found that creativity assessments aren't random — they are actually highly structured and consistent.

There are two general definitions of creativity that people use. Culture dictates part of why people use one definition or another. But we found differences within the United States as well. In the United States, 70 percent of people used one definition, but 30 percent used another. The two definitions of creativity are:

- 70 percent of Americans believe creativity means that something is new, often infeasible, and "socially horrifying" — a term used by Malcom Gladwell to mean that an idea is not widely accepted because it breaks social norms and conventions.

- 30 percent of Americans believe creativity means that something is new but also feasible, appealing to the masses, and socially acceptable.

The two examples that follow help further describe these two definitions, and the conflict we feel over them.

An article in the *Wall Street Journal* titled the "The Innovator's Enigma" chronicled a mystery. The article asked how the CEO of Procter and Gamble, Bob McDonald, could label ZzzQuil — basically NyQuil without the cold medicine — as a breakthrough new product category, when competitors already had similar products on the market. Furthermore, the article noted that a disappointed and disillusioned portfolio manager called ZzzQuil merely "incremental" and "derivative."

Another article, this one in *The New Yorker,* showcased differences in how people define creativity. In Malcolm Gladwell's account of Steve Jobs, entitled "The Tweaker," Gladwell notes that "Jobs was someone who took other people's ideas and changed them." In an earlier article, Malcolm Gladwell described true creativity as "socially horrifying" — in that it challenges convention and so isn't widely accepted. Gladwell's account of Steve Jobs seems to be in stark contrast to a *Fast Company* article calling Jobs the Picasso of our generation.

Both the innovator's enigma and the tweaker show our definitions of creativity battling it out for supremacy. I'll start with Malcolm Gladwell's definition. The first way to define creativity is: *creativity equals new.* That's right, to most people in the United States, *creativity* and *novelty* are synonyms. People who use this definition think that creative ideas should have a function, but this is not as critical for creativity. What *is* critical for creativity is novelty. One marker of novelty is that it breaks convention, so it can be socially horrifying. Another marker of novelty can be that you did something so difficult to do that nobody else had done it before. Malcolm Gladwell notes that Jobs didn't *invent* any of the technology he used to develop the iPhone — he just put the pieces together. The new inventions happened largely at PARC, where Jobs bragged that he "stole" various technologies.

So if most people in the United States believe that creative ideas are new ideas, what do they think of ideas that are conventional, appeal to the masses, have a big brand, are easy to make, and are fashionable? What would Malcolm Gladwell think of ZzzQuil? For most people who share his view of creativity, saying that an idea is for a mass market or is widely socially accepted kills their feeling of fit. In other words, if an idea has a big brand and everyone likes it, how can it be distinctive?

But to a Bob McDonald kind of decision maker, ZzzQuil is creative because it repurposes the NyQuil brand, is highly feasible to make, and is easily marketable to the masses. In contrast, to a Malcolm Gladwell kind of thinker, ZzzQuil lacks creativity because it just repurposes a brand and does not create a new product. ZzzQuil is essentially Benadryl, a drug that has been on the market for decades. All P&G did was put a hefty price tag on it and give it a new name. And to a person who cares about novelty, big brands just emphasize that a product is endorsed by the masses and so not distinctive. So my guess is that Malcolm Gladwell would not find ZzzQuil to be creative at all.

Have you ever had an argument with someone where the two of you simply value different things? Maybe you prioritize cost savings highly while your coworker values brand management. When you need to make a tradeoff (e.g., pay more money to advertise the brand), this discussion can get very heated. It's going to feel personal — like the other person doesn't like you. When we hold different values than others we have to collaborate with, emotional conflict is inevitable. And studies show that little good comes from having emotional conflict.

And when it comes to creativity, emotional conflict can be highly charged. This is because we both love and hate creativity, so our feelings about it are intense. The portfolio manager exhibited disillusionment and disappointment with the CEO's decision to manufacture ZzzQuil. How would you feel if the company you worked for said it wanted creativity and innovation — and then chose to adopt products you thought were boring and incremental? You might very well think the managers in your organization were hypocrites.

People have strong feelings about creativity because they spend a lot of time and energy on creative pursuits. We can even define ourselves by our creative works. When others disagree with us and say that our ideas are not actually that creative, it can feel awful. I spoke with a designer who said he felt like he was going crazy. He said "I did something really unique — that nobody had ever done — and my manager just shrugged her shoulders and said, 'This is linear — I don't see the new factor here.' How could she say that? Am I going nuts? Am I just stupid? How could she fail to see how new this is?"

In addition, when decision makers choose to pursue ideas that we don't think are creative, it feels like they rejected our work in favor of something dumb. Either way, we feel disrespected.

My point is not to say that one definition of creativity is better than the other. Both definitions have value and both have blind spots. Instead, I'm contending that people engaging in a creative effort will feel disheartened and rejected when the way they are defining creativity does not fit what others are looking for.

Classical studies in social psychology found that when you tell people in a group to brainstorm ideas, many will exhibit what is termed "evaluation apprehension" — a fear of being judged harshly for expressing a new idea. One of the reasons could be that ideas that appeal to a why/potential way of thinking might not appeal to a how/best way of thinking, and vice versa.

In other words, I think people have been having conflict around creativity without a real sense of true communication. I recommend you take the two steps below to diminish conflict and aid communication regarding creative ideas.

Communicate: Understand how your definition of creativity may differ from others'

If you want to diminish the conflict and start to truly communicate, you should determine which kind of person you are — a Malcolm Gladwell (why/potential) type or a CEO Bob McDonald (how/best) type. Below is a survey. Please rate the extent to which you think the following statements are important to something being creative. That is, how important *to you* is this feature to a product being creative? (1 = not at all, 6 = extremely)

1. People had to think really differently to come up with it.
2. It applies a solution to a completely different area.
3. It is easy to use.
4. Those who make it have a good reputation.
5. It is in fashion.
6. It is for a big market.
7. It is a big brand.
8. It is easy to make.

Everyone tends to answer that numbers 1 and 2 of the survey indicate that something is highly creative — so they score above a 4. But if your average score for items 3–8 was below a 4 on the scale, then you are more like Malcolm Gladwell (e.g., why/potential). If your average score for items 3–8 was above a 4, you have more of a how/best or Bob McDonald view of creativity.

Now that you know how you define creativity, you might be surprised to know that others in your organization might have the exact opposite definition. If you rated numbers 3–8 above a 4 on creativity, you are in the minority in the United States. And you're probably also in the minority among designers and other idea generators in your organization. But you are not in the minority among decision makers.

In other words, it's important to acknowledge that your definition may differ from others'. And if you gave these attributes below a 4, it is important to acknowledge that people in decision-making roles might not agree with you. So you would be in the minority among decision makers.

The next step is to realize that no one definition is right or better. Each definition actually has a blind spot. The why/potential way of defining creativity might not recognize lucrative opportunities like ZzzQuil. The how/best way of defining creative opportunity might not recognize early-stage opportunity. You can't have it both ways. You can't define creativity in a how/best way and expect your employees to give you what you want if they have a why/potential kind of view. And you can't expect early-stage creative ideas to perfectly fit your how/best view of creativity. They just don't.

Communicate: Make your definition explicit to employees. The first question you need to ask yourself is: do you want innovation with the why/potential kind of creativity? If you don't — if you want the decision-maker, how/best kind of innovation — there is nothing wrong with that. Just remember that using the word *innovation* could confuse and annoy your people.

I remember giving a keynote address at an internal corporate innovation workshop. After my talk about the importance of creativity, the company founders spent a good deal of time talking about the good old days, when the company had several breakthrough products that redefined the industry and put them on the map. They mentioned being puzzled and frustrated at why the company couldn't replicate their breakthrough products from the '80s. Management then issued a call to employees to be more innovative and to push the boundaries, but to also understand the strong feasibility constraints the company now faced. Since it hadn't had a breakthrough in more than thirty years, the company was starting to hurt financially, and so they had fewer resources to spend on innovation.

After my talk, I sat in the audience with the engineers and designers, and I had a chance to hear their side of the story. "Management is full of hypocrites," they said. "They all say they want something new and different, but all they care about is whether they can immediately sell a design to the masses. Anything new that needs development will automatically get rejected because they don't see it as feasible."

When I later met with the corporate leaders to debrief, I asked them if they really wanted creativity and innovation. They told me, unsurprisingly, that creativity and innovation were their passion. Furthermore, they told me, for them, the writing was on the wall. They were either going to be creative or die. They were frustrated and frankly disheartened that the engineers weren't being creative. Both sides were unhappy over a lack of creativity.

Would those same employees have had the same reaction if leaders at this company had said, "Listen, we want to move fast and be innovative but right now, the kind of innovation we want is ZzzQuil — to repackage a product that already exists in a way that we can quickly and feasibly bring to market. Right now in our history, we need immediate revenue and we can't afford to take risks."

Or maybe your company wants both. Most companies that want the why/potential *and* how/best kinds of creativity make one critical mistake. They don't tell employees what this really means. If you want both kinds of creativity, it means that you really want about 80 percent of the how/best kind of creativity and only 20 percent of the why/potential kind. In other words, you need and want more of the how/best creativity. If you give your people free time to work on innovative products, ask them to split the time accordingly — on how/best kinds of ideas (repurposing a product you already have, or marketing an existing product in a new way) and why/potential kinds of ideas (developing a product your company currently does not offer or that is new to the market). You can even tell them to try and split their free time 80/20.

In sum, making your definitions of creativity explicit, but also telling your people how much time to devote to each type, can help you seem like less of a hypocrite and more authentic and real.

CHECKS WITHOUT BALANCES

If I had to nominate one main reason why corporate America is stagnating and failing to embrace creative change, I'd need just one phrase: all checks, no balances. In most large organizations that want innovation, the power to make the decision to innovate is given to a relatively small group of people. That decision-making group or person does not have to collaborate or compromise with the person or group generating the idea. That decision-making group or person can trump the designer, company founder — or whoever is responsible for developing the idea — by mandating design changes or killing projects.

What happens to the innovation process when people with a how/best mindset have total control over it? The how/best mindset loves reducing uncertainty. What reduces uncertainty in the face of innovation (aside from rejecting creative ideas)? Bureaucracy, red tape, highly structured and formalized processes where idea generators can't say *boo* without decision-making approval. These things make the person in a how/best mindset feel more in control and less anxious. Unfortunately, they also kill early-stage creative ideas.

Robert Cooper is an academic who developed the idea of stage-gate processes — a mechanized process to manage innovation. If you visit his website, you see a video where he talks about his innovation journey. He begins with a story of his first job out of college, where he worked for a small, successful company. This small company made a terrible decision to pivot and to develop a new product with a different application. He then notes that the company made even more mistakes and eventually went bankrupt. To fix this kind of problem, he notes that companies need a highly structured process to ensure that innovations are of high quality. This is where the stage-gate process comes in.

Stage-gate processes are varied, but the basic principle is that you have some kind of decision-making team (think of them as adults) that keep those developing products (think of them as kids) in check. The way this works is that the "adult" team decides which products have a wow factor — products that meet unarticulated customer needs. After doing due diligence and vetting an idea thoroughly, the decision-making team is put in charge of closely monitoring the activities of a cross-functional group to develop the product.

Then the cross-functional team has to meet with the decision-making team through various stages, and their product has to meet certain metrics to go through the gate to receive funding for the next stage of development. Some companies I've worked with have up to ten or twenty stages and gates for just one project.

Critically, the decision-making team in a stage-gate model is not involved in the creative process in any meaningful way. They don't watch the progression and give constant input. They aren't part of the process other than to look at the end result and decide.

I have to say that when it comes to the how/best kind of creative ideas, stage gates work beautifully. That being said, I don't think you need to overdo it and have too many stages and gates. The basic process really does enforce quality control.

But when it comes to the why/potential kind of creative ideas, stage gates are all checks and no balances:

- Having decision makers decide which ideas have a wow factor? *Check!* Decision makers want proven ideas and don't tolerate ideas with poor metrics. Ideas with poor metrics aren't even creative to them by definition (even if everyone else disagrees, or the metrics are fake).

- Having decision makers watch from on high and interact with the developers only when they choose? *Check!* Developers often encounter problems or bugs and need to make quick decisions about whether to use budget money to pivot or not.

- Deciding that ideas pass through gates and receive future funding only if they succeed in proving value? *Check!* What if you failed, but in doing so learned that all you needed to do was pivot one more time to find the value? From a stage-gate perspective, because you needed to pivot, in effect you failed, so your idea does not warrant funding for the next stage.

When it comes to highly creative ideas, stage-gate processes tend to be too rigid and not well suited to creative change or the process of developing highly creative ideas.

Balance Your Checks:
Accountability for Creativity

In my field we used to believe that decision makers faced a dilemma — a no-win situation. They had to choose either creative options that had poor metrics and face potential derision if ideas failed, or choose known options with great metrics that might not solve the problem nearly as well in the long term. What my research team and I have found is that decision makers don't actually face a dilemma at all.

To a decision maker, ideas with poor metrics aren't creative to begin with. Our research shows that decision makers with the Bob McDonald kind of creativity believe that ideas with proven wide appeal and market potential are creative. In fact, we've found that the mere fact that an idea has wide market potential indicates to a how/best decision maker that the idea is creative — even if competitors have been producing similar products for years. This means that if you tell your executives to choose creative ideas — hoping for the Malcolm Gladwell kind of creativity — they aren't going to give it to you. They won't endorse ideas that could make them look bad if they fail. Therefore your portfolio of ideas chosen by decision makers may include some new ideas, but the kind of ideas you really want will be filtered out. So giving mandates to your managers to select creative ideas is unlikely to change the kinds of ideas they will endorse.

My research team and I have learned that consumers and even designers have a more accurate, less biased way of viewing creative ideas. That's because consumers and designers are less likely to have a how/best kind of mindset. They don't care if ideas are highly feasible, for example.

The solution then is to create a two-step process of idea selection instead of a one-step process where you give decision makers a set of ideas and tell them to choose some that are creative. The first step is to use the wisdom of crowds (WOC) methodology outlined in Chapter 4. Use WOC to rate the quality and creativity of all your ideas. Then get rid of all the ideas with low quality ratings and tell decision makers to choose a certain number of high- and low-creativity ideas.

Critically in this process, decision makers are not judging which ideas are creative. And they have a mandate to choose at least some ideas that others (e.g., consumers, designers) view as creative that they might not. This second point is important — by telling decision makers to choose at least some ideas that others view as creative, you are giving them a way to cover their butts. They can say, "I don't see the value in this idea, but I had no choice but to advance it." In other words, you are creating checks with balances. You only have checks in a system that leaves decision makers open to criticism if they choose a creative idea on their own. You have checks and balances when you give decision makers an out, when you let them say "I told you so" if the idea fails, but allow them to take credit if the idea succeeds.

Balance Your Checks: Give Joint Decision-Making Authority to Managers and Creatives

Rob Cook won numerous awards for software products, both at startup companies and at Pixar, including the first Oscar ever given for software. Cook was Pixar's vice president of software development when he and his colleagues developed RenderMan, a product used in making all of Pixar's films as well as twenty-four of the last twenty-six films to win the visual effects Oscar. As you can well imagine, he has gleaned some pretty important insights over the years. One of those insights came from working closely with the filmmakers and seeing how they were able to be so creative while meeting deadlines. He realized that much of what Pixar was doing had parallels to the way startups and even established companies could develop creative products.

Every Pixar film has a director and a producer. Directors are in charge of all creative aspects of the story. Producers are in charge of the budget, the schedule, meeting deadlines, and cost management. The director "owns" the movie but not the budget; the producer "owns" the budget but not the movie. Neither trumps the other. The director can't say, "Too bad, I'm going to spend more money anyhow," and the producer can't say, "Too bad, you need to cut this scene." This kind of relationship works because each provides a check and balance for the other.

Brad Bird directed *The Incredibles* and John Walker was the producer. *The Incredibles* was the first movie Pixar produced with a full cast of human characters. It required inventing technology for simulating human movement and realistic skin, clothing, and hair. Brad Bird admitted that he "had the knees of [the studio] trembling under the weight" of the film, given the technical challenges. For example, one of the main characters — Violet — is shy and has long hair that she hides behind. There was just one problem: no one had ever managed to figure out how to simulate long hair before.

Walker noted that "It brought the production to its knees for a long time because we kept trying and kept trying and kept trying ... and couldn't do it. Finally, we had a summit where the big-brained guys who run the simulator, the thing that makes the hair move, finally just sat across the table and said, 'You know, John, I've got to tell you, long hair is theoretical at this point.' Wow.

Time out! Theoretical? The movie goes out in less than a year. What do you mean, it's theoretical?"

So Walker told Bird that they needed to give Violet short hair in order to get the movie done. But for Bird, Violet's hair was essential to her character, so he wouldn't give in; he put his foot down and fought. And so the pressure was on the simulation engineers, but they rose to the occasion and, in the end, Violet's hair looked wonderful.

But Bird didn't win every argument with Walker. For example, he really wanted Jack-Jack — the baby in the family — to turn into goo at the end of the movie. But it would have taken two months to develop the right look and texture for goo. Bird and Walker argued, but after two months, Bird conceded and agreed to cut the goo idea.

By giving the director and producer equal power, Pixar avoided shortcutting the tension between creativity and efficiency, and that led to a good balance between the two and often to a new solution. Rob realized that this approach was relevant to more than just movies. He had seen it at work in the software startups he had run and in his software team at Pixar. The underlying principle was the same, and an important principle for any team trying to build creative new products.

When I heard Cook's insight, I realized that directors have more of a why/potential mindset, while producers have more of a how/best mindset. When it comes to developing a creative product, both concerns constantly compete. But instead of structuring the task to let one concern win (how/best or why/potential), you can create two equally powerful roles that balance the two.

At Better Place, the why/potential view ran amok. Shai Agassi might have fared better if he'd partnered with a savvy how/best kind of leader who could have balanced him out. Similarly, when it comes to early-stage creativity, stage-gate processes tend to be out of balance. For example, you may have heard the phrase "Fail fast and often." Robert Cooper can say failure is good, but he has created a system that does not view failure in a balanced way. In a stage-gate world, failure doesn't mean learning or improvement, failure is just a reason to reject an idea and to fail to pass it through the gate! How can you get more funding if your idea failed the last gate test?

So use your stage-gate processes for only incrementally creative ideas. You can use the measuring system developed in Chapter 4 and have your employees tell you which ideas best fit in this bucket. But for those ideas that get a 3 and above rating for creativity, you can structure their development quite differently — the way Pixar does. Instead of having one leader, you can assign two — one leader who heads the creative process, and a second leader who manages the budget and any regulatory concerns. Your budget leader can serve as an ambassador with legal and manufacturing and can bring outside concerns to the team early on (rather than later in the process, when it is too late to make big changes).

Importantly — and this part is key — this budget manager *must collaborate and come to a joint decision with the creative leader.* For there to be checks and also balances in the system, the budget manager must not have the power to trump the creative team leader — nor can the creative team leader trump the manager. The budget manager can't mandate that the creative leader change the product, and the creative leader can't generate ideas forever. What you want is healthy debate, disagreement, and negotiation between the two leaders — not meetings whenever the budget leader feels like they're warranted. You want to create a partnership between two leaders with equal power so that you have checks but also balances.

I'm proposing that rather than assessing risk, developing a

stage-gate process, and creating a bureaucratic organization — with red tape that is risk averse — you have another choice: Let the creatives share the reins with the management.

You may have heard the term *skunk works,* meaning an entity or division that is physically separate from the larger organization, often in a building housing scientists and engineers whose role is to develop new and breakthrough products and services. Skunk works are still in wide use today. But the history of many skunk works reeks of the theme "all checks, no balances" when it comes to innovation.

The term *skunk works* was first featured in a *Li'l Abner* comic strip as a ramshackle factory located in the middle of nowhere where they made "skonk oil." A combination of dead skunks and worn shoes, it had no clear purpose, but it smelled so bad that it killed scores of locals. In the modern interpretation, skunk works are structured such that "creative types" are ostracized from the political and social workings of the broader organization. Skunk works employees often have no decision-making authority over their budget or which products are brought to market — presumably because they are thought to be too out of touch to make good decisions about the direction the company should take.

Unsurprisingly, there are many examples of skunk works developing breakthrough products that were never implemented by the parent company. Perhaps the most famous example was at Xerox PARC. Xerox's management ignored the new products developed by PARC that other companies, like Apple and Microsoft, developed into billion-dollar businesses. This happened because the decision makers at Xerox had complete control over any product developed at PARC. To quote one executive, "The corporate leaders at Xerox back in the day were just not interested in the potential of the ideas at PARC. It wasn't their thing."

But skunk works function beautifully at places like Lockheed Martin. Kelly Johnson, a legendary Lockheed engineer who rose to a VP role later in his career, wrote the book on successful skunk works. Rule number 1 in Kelly's 14 Rules & Practices is "The skunk works manager must be delegated practically complete control of his program."

What I'm suggesting is a hybrid version of this practice. Delegate complete control to two decision-making counterparts with opposite concerns. Then let them have the hard conversations and allow them to strike the right balance.

In recent years, it has become more and more common for large organizations to hire chief innovation officers (CIOs). The role of the CIO is to manage all aspects of innovation within the organization. When I speak confidentially to leaders in these roles, they call themselves "monkeys." Some say they are the creatives who are ignored by CEOs. One executive told me she was "patted on the head and told by the CEO, 'This idea is great, but it just isn't feasible.'"

I think that having a CIO is a great idea. But having the role of CIO without having the power to act on your instincts is just another check without a balance for early-stage creative ideas. If organizations really care about blue-sky innovation, the CIO role should be structured differently. The CIO might collaborate with the CFO, for example, to have authority to jointly decide which ideas should be implemented without interference from the CEO. The point is that creative change is a difficult road for anyone. Sharing power between two roles with opposite interests can help create balance because each keeps the other in check.

In sum, giving top-tier executives complete power over innovation won't help you develop the next big breakthrough. The truth is, in my experience, most executives don't have the motivation or skills to promote creative change. Even if they do have the motivation, my research shows that a focus on money, metrics, and a how/best mindset (instilled by most MBA programs and corporate contexts) will kill their ability to recognize early-stage ideas as great opportunities. That said, executives have a valuable perspective. But so do idea generators, designers, and your creatives. Instead of prioritizing one over the other, let them share power. Let them duke it out.

7

Overcome the Bias against Creative Leadership

LET'S RETURN TO BOB McDONALD FOR A MOMENT.
Around 2011, as Procter and Gamble's CEO, McDonald was hailed as a creative leader. He described innovation as a major strategic priority for his company when he said, "We know from our history that while promotions may win quarters, innovation wins decades." He encouraged idea generation from all corners of the company. Specifically, under his reign the company spent nearly $2 billion annually on R&D (50 percent more than its closest competitor). P&G had honed the Connect + Develop crowdsourcing website, where suppliers and consumers are encouraged to suggest new product ideas. By all accounts, the ideas P&G had access to and the funds to develop them were surging.

But at this point, after reading this book, do you think encouraging employees and others to generate ideas was enough? Not according to P&G, which replaced McDonald with A. G. Lafley after the company's performance declined under McDonald's leadership.

A. G. Lafley was the former P&G CEO who stepped down in 2009 when P&G's profits were on the rise. Due to his prior performance at P&G, Lafley was hailed as a "strategic visionary and an innovation guru." One journalist compared the return of A. G.

Lafley to P&G to the return of Steve Jobs to Apple. So when Lafley took over in 2013, he was seen as a creative leader too. But was he? Not according to James Surowiecki at *The New Yorker*, who noted that Lafley steered the company away from new product launches and sold off less profitable businesses, and under Lafley's leadership P&G's stock prices underperformed the market.

P&G is not alone — most companies and the people in them struggle to recognize true creative leadership. But why? Could it be that just as we can hold an implicit bias against creative ideas, could we also hold an implicit bias against selecting creative people as leaders?

Ask any leader and she or he will tell you, *absolutely not!* IBM conducted a survey of over 1,500 CEOs and identified creativity as the number-one leadership competency to win in the future. When asked to name the one attribute CEOs need most to succeed in today's turbulent economy, Michael Dell, CEO of Dell Inc., replied, "curiosity." So clearly, if the number-one leadership competency is creativity and the curiosity to cultivate it, then people are sure to be promoted to leadership roles if they exhibit creativity, right?

Jordan Cohen, a manager at Pfizer, was featured in *Business-Week, Fast Company,* and *Harvard Business Review* for developing PfizerWorks — a process to get twenty-four-hour feedback from users. How did Cohen get buy-in to develop his idea? He didn't. He hid his efforts for almost two years to gain enough time to hone the service and to prove the concept. At the time, he was the chief innovation officer of the company.

Priya Kannan-Narasimhan interviewed Silicon Valley innovators at companies that lauded innovation and creativity. Can you guess how they got buy-in for early-stage innovations? They didn't. In fact, like Jordan Cohen, they hid their projects. One manager in a large Silicon Valley firm who participated in the study summed it up beautifully, "A very common tactic here is: Do stuff under the radar as long as you can, get a prototype to show, and then start showing people — and then you know you can get through some of the initial 'Oh, that'll never work.'"

What are innovators hiding from? Creativity research before 2011 says that everyone believes creative types are intelligent, witty, fun, charismatic, and interesting. So if you took this research to heart, you might describe yourself as a *creative* problem solver versus a *practical* problem solver on your résumé to help you find a job. Jack Goncalo and I tested this idea (but never published the data). We chose the exact same résumé but varied it only on whether the candidate said he was a creative problem solver or a practical problem solver. Turns out, framing your problem-solving ability as "creative" versus "practical" will, all other things being equal, make others view you as a better-qualified job candidate.

So maybe labeling yourself as creative is a good thing. One CEO told me that she resented the fact that a subordinate said she wasn't creative because she was so efficient at implementation. The evidence suggests that *everyone* loves creative thinkers, and we dearly want to label ourselves as creative.

But do we really?

One hallmark of a creative person is, of course, that she comes up with creative ideas. And you already know our complicated relationship with creative ideas. Creative ideas have uncertain feasibility; we just don't know if they are reliable and useful in all the ways we hope. So just as we admit to loving creative ideas while we hide our hate of them, could we also admit to loving but hiding our hate of creative *people*? In turn, is that why creative people hide from *us*?

If this is true, then labeling yourself as a creative thinker is all well and good, until you produce a creative idea that is uncertain. Once you add uncertainty into the mix by expressing your creative idea, your reputation is now on the line — especially when it comes to leadership.

THE TRICKY RELATIONSHIP BETWEEN
LEADERSHIP AND CREATIVITY

Bob Nardelli rose through the ranks at GE during the Jack Welch era, which had zero tolerance for nonperformers. Given this stellar pedigree, Nardelli should have become one of the great leaders of our time, right? Well, not quite. Nardelli did not meet with great success as CEO of Home Depot, nor later at Chrysler. But he's not alone — other leaders with top-notch résumés have had disastrous failures, too. For example, after heading Andersen Consulting — now Accenture — George Shaheen was installed as the CEO of Webvan, one of the largest startups during the dot-com bubble. You would think that one of the most successful business consultants in the world would make a great leader, but, as it turned out, Webvan did not succeed.

How do we choose our leaders? There are two ways. We choose leaders whom we view as expert, and who know the key strategies that their groups need in order to succeed at important tasks. But the second (and more common) way we choose leaders is by employing stereotypes. That is, we look to see what traits a person has, and if those traits match our personal beliefs about leadership, we usually peg her or him as a leader. We believe leaders are intelligent, strong, charismatic, masculine, tyrannical, dedicated, and attractive. In other words, our stereotypes concerning leaders tell us that we need to promote and follow the strong person who seems to fit all the criteria.

Notice that our stereotypes of leadership don't have much to say about creativity directly. There is no reference to curiosity either. So what happens to our reputations as leaders if we tell others our creative ideas?

Jack Goncalo and I recruited Dishan Kamdar of the Indian School of Business to do some research with us at a large oil refinery in India. This particular company was very proud of its ability to promote creative ingenuity. We examined a group of engineers who were all responsible for discovering new ways to keep the plant running efficiently. We asked the engineers' supervisors to rate each engineer on two abilities: the extent to which they generated creative ideas, and their overall leadership potential. What we found surprised us. Instead of finding a positive link between the generation of creative ideas and leadership potential, the two were *negatively* correlated. This means that the more creative ideas engineers generated, the less their supervisors perceived them to be leaderlike. We have since replicated this same finding in at least two other companies.

People are punished for expressing creative ideas in America, too. My colleagues and I went into two Ivy League universities to conduct a similar study. We found that students who scored high on a creative ability task were less likely to be seen as leaders by peers in their study groups. We conducted another study and assigned students to pitch either a creative or a practical idea to an observer. We learned that when students pitched the creative idea, they were seen as less leaderlike by observers than when they pitched the practical idea. We replicated this finding even in contexts where people were expected to brainstorm, and when the creative and practical ideas expressed were of equal quality.

I later dug deeper into our general beliefs about creative people and found that we think creative types are smart and fun. But people in business contexts also peg creatives as being naive and too disorganized to get things done and efficiently implement ideas. In some pilot studies I ran, I found that if you brainstormed *many* ideas in front of others (relative to selling a *single* idea) you were seen as inefficient, lacking business savvy, and less leaderlike.

In contrast, we want our leaders to know the answers. We want our leaders to be experts. We want our leaders to make us feel *less uncertain* about the world, not *more uncertain.* And we care whether our leaders can execute tasks efficiently.

If you were to follow our stereotypes of leadership to a T, guess who would fit them perfectly? Donald Trump. Even though four of Trump's businesses filed for Chapter 11 bankruptcy reorganization, he has no previous political experience, and he is described by some as a bully, as of this writing he was the Republican presidential candidate for 2016. Remember, we always love the feeling of fit, and will forgive people a lot if we think they have it. For a flamboyant businessperson like Trump, because he fits our stereotypes so well, research shows that we will be less critical of him even if he ultimately fails. In other words, autocratic narcissists perfectly fit our old-school definition of leadership.

Where do these stereotypes come from? They come from the history we learned in grade school about kings, tyrants, and warlords. We learn them from TV shows like *The Sopranos* and from movies like *The Wolf of Wall Street,* where autocratic narcissists are lauded. Of course, this stereotype of leadership plays well in the media and in history books. These leadership stories are interesting and so remembered and repeated (often as cautionary tales). But the truth is, these stereotypes are woefully out of date.

In today's world, we have less and less use for purely autocratic leaders. Why? Because to be an effective autocrat, you need to be the most expert person in the group, and you need to know the answers to productively tell people what to do.

But in today's complex world, where you need deep expertise to know anything about any domain, nobody can truly know all the answers. In contrast, it's a sense of humility — not taking credit for knowing the answers — that promotes effective leadership. Therefore, there is a mismatch between our stereotypes and the traits that leaders actually need to lead effectively in today's world. The old-school stereotypes of leadership often move us to promote the wrong people into leadership roles. I believe these antiquated stereotypes of leadership are a major source of the creativity crisis in America.

Where is the evidence that today's leaders lack the skills to make creative change?

Let me give you an example. One large company approached me with an internal white paper that they did not want others to read. The white paper showed that leaders in this organization were highly proficient at communicating, problem solving, and organizing. Unfortunately, these leaders also received low scores on creative thinking. In short, these leaders could execute well, but they could not easily adapt to new situations. This reality was holding the company back.

In his groundbreaking book, *Leadership BS,* Jeffrey Pfeffer notes the overwhelming evidence that those we elect or appoint into leadership positions lack the skills to make creative change and fail themselves, their customers, stockholders, and employees.

SOCIETAL CONTRIBUTORS TO THE CREATIVITY CRISIS

By the way, the creativity crisis isn't happening only in corporate organizations, it's also happening in American schools. And the data suggests that the problem is bigger than you might think. Kyung Hee Kim at the College of William and Mary examined a sample of 272,599 students in kindergarten through twelfth grade. She identified that millennials had significantly lower creative-thinking test scores relative to earlier generations. Millennials weren't generating as many ideas, and they weren't exhibiting as much motivation to explain them either. According to this research, hiring more millennials because you think younger people have stronger creative ability won't help your organization become more creative.

So why have students' creative-thinking scores declined over time? Ken Robinson's TED talk — the most-popular TED talk ever — does a good job of explaining why. Early in his talk, titled "Do schools kill creativity?" Robinson says, "I believe this passionately, that we don't grow into creativity, we grow out of it. Or rather, we get educated out of it." And he notes Picasso's famous quote that "all children are born artists." But then he says, "Every education system on Earth has the same hierarchy of subjects. Every one. At the top are mathematics and languages, then the humanities, and at the bottom are the arts." Then he notes that there "isn't an education system on the planet that teaches dance every day to children the way we teach them mathematics." Basically, he equates creativity with the arts and notes that creativity is not a teaching priority for most schools. He then asserts that schools should devote more time to teaching the creative arts, like dance.

But this is the exact reason that educational administrators give for *not* including more creativity in the classroom. One review paper showed that teachers believe creativity happens mainly in the arts and involves doing something new that doesn't necessarily have a practical purpose or use — so it is not essential.

Put your FAB (fit, aha, broaden) hat on. Now that you know how sticky the status quo bias is, do you think Ken Robinson's talk would rally educational administrators to change? Do you think his plea would make educational administrators feel the failure? Or does he make the classic mistake of telling people what the status quo is, note that everybody is doing it, only to then say, *Don't do it?* This might be the most popular TED talk of all time, but it's more likely to further reinforce the status quo than to change it.

Here is the problem for business executives. Every executive who grew up in the United States has been taught by an elementary school teacher. So if elementary school teachers equate creativity with the arts — which they believe are important, but not essential for education — what message do you think teachers send to the next generation of leaders? When conducting seminars on creativity, executives will often tell me, "We aren't artists. Why do we need to learn about creativity?" So the bias against creativity (creativity is for artists, not businesspeople) that I often see in corporate America appears to have strong roots in U.S. schools.

People have blamed standardized tests and No Child Left Behind for the decline in creativity in U.S. schools. People have blamed teachers as well. But I think blaming teachers is a mistake. They are embedded in a larger, autocratic system. The system pushes teachers to reduce the focus on creativity in order to teach students to take standardized tests. So who controls the system?

Educational administrators do — the school boards, principals, politicians, and administrative staff who make the policies. They tell the teachers how to structure education, and thus they kick creativity out of the curriculum, not teachers. And given what we know about leaders lacking creativity in corporate America, why would we think it's any different in education? The people we promote to leadership positions in our schools are likely as how/best oriented as the people we promote to leadership positions in corporate America.

I believe the creativity crisis America faces stems from a lack of creative leadership. In today's complex, ever-changing world, you need to understand how to make creative change in an organization to be an effective leader. But the leaders we select today in our schools and corporations are often promoted based on an out-of-date stereotyped image of what leadership should look like. That old stereotype is no longer relevant for a new world of increased complexity, where creative thinking by a diverse group of people is every bit as important as efficient execution.

I believe our current inability to recognize creative leadership is sowing the seeds of a creativity crisis in America. The good news is that we can retrain ourselves to recognize creative leadership. If you could learn how to recognize the difference between the antiquated stereotype and the new model of creative leadership, then you could more accurately identify the kinds of leaders with the skills to recognize and embrace productive new directions.

In sum, if, as a nation, we want creativity, we need to disrupt our long-held stereotypes of leadership. We need to follow a process of creative change that includes recognizing our current definition of leadership, understanding when this definition gets us into trouble, and then learning to expand the definition to become more productive. To that end, I've developed a three-step process to identify creative leaders in your organization.

Step 1: Diagnose Your Definition of Leadership

Below is the transcript of a decision-making meeting, adapted from an actual business situation. Executives in this meeting came from many different disciplines and were charged with choosing a system to make all information electronic in the American healthcare industry. In 2012, the American healthcare market was estimated to total $3 trillion, and it was increasing at a rate of 4 percent per year, so it accounted for roughly 15 percent of U.S. GDP. This decision had massive economic implications.

As you read through this discussion, see if you can identify the leader.

RICK: Our goal is to make a decision today. We have four options to choose from. We can either go with what exists, Option 1, which is not our mandate, or we can choose Option 2, Option 3, or Option 4.

JIM: Before we start, it's essential that we keep in mind the feasibility constraints we face. We need to coordinate among multiple institutions, states, and across many kinds of technological platforms. We also need to choose a solution we can implement relatively quickly without spending our entire budget in case we need to tweak later.

TOM: Thanks, Jim, but I think the feasibility issues are secondary to patient privacy concerns. If we get this thing wrong, we could have a bioterrorism situation on our hands or we could dismantle the entire health network as we know it.

SUSAN: I agree — patient privacy is key. If we lose that, we have no solution. We are in an Internet security war with hackers from China and elsewhere. What happens if the security in place now fails to handle the security issues we already face? I understand Option 1 isn't advisable, but until Internet security improves, I don't see us having any other choice.

[The group is silent for a moment.]

JADA: Let me ask you something, Susan. Why is Option 1 a good solution? What problem are we trying to solve?

SUSAN: Well, I think it's pretty obvious that Option 1 doesn't solve a problem, but it keeps us from having another kind of problem.

JIM: I see the problem as multidimensional. The ultimate goal is to reduce costs in the system. This would also help patients and physicians quickly access data, and that would improve the quality of healthcare. So I guess the point of the solution is to bring value to the patient and the hospitals.

RICK: I agree that the whole point of this committee is to do something. If we do nothing the entire system suffers. But, personally, I think Option 4 is really way off in the future. We would have to ramp up the entire system, and that simply isn't feasible. Option 3 is also a stretch, but I don't think Option 2 is enough. Option 2 will simply not allow for a wide enough impact. So I don't see a clear solution here.

TOM: I agree. All the solutions we face have some benefits, but huge downsides. I believe our role is to minimize the downsides. None of the solutions on the table allows us to do that.

JADA: So how do we make this work? You have discussed how it doesn't work. How can we use what we have to make it feasible and impactful?

JIM: Well, I suppose one option could be to combine solutions. What if we combined the best of Option 2 with Option 3? We can think of this as a progression — we could even add Option 4 as a future final step in the chain of progression. That way, our plan would have a short-term implementation strategy, with a long-term trajectory.

RICK: That's a great idea, Jim!

TOM: I think it's reasonable.

SUSAN: I still think we need to be very careful with respect to security concerns.

RICK: Great. Let's talk about exactly what this new option would look like . . .

Who is the person *most* responsible for shaping the creativity in the meeting? In other words, who would you peg as the main creative leader of this discussion?

You might say Rick was the leader because he kicked off the discussion, identified the options, and later guided the team toward fleshing out the solution. You might say Jim was the leader because he was the one to emphasize the group's mandate to improve the quality of healthcare, and ultimately generated the solution the group chose.

If you chose either Rick or Jim as the leader, then you might define leadership as simply "managing the meeting," or "knowing the answer on future direction." But all these kinds of leadership are very much in line with the old-school stereotypes we use to identify leaders. So if you chose either of these people, then you might fall prey to discounting creative leadership when you see it.

There is another way to view leadership. In this alternative view, knowing the answer is great, but just because you have technical skill or smarts doesn't mean you can cultivate creativity in the group. For that matter, merely reiterating the group goal or purpose is helpful, but it does not necessarily motivate others to generate creative solutions. Enforcing an agenda and summarizing options might make you a good line manager, but you aren't actually leading the group in a *creative* direction.

So who was responsible for shaping the creative direction of the meeting? Who pushed the group to open up and think differently? I would say that Jada was the creative leader in this group. It is true that Jada didn't know the answer. It is true that Jada didn't structure the meeting. But by asking questions, Jada disrupted the direction of the meeting. She disrupted the group from choosing the status quo. This also opened up a space for Jim to have the idea that the team ultimately chose. Jada didn't have the creative idea, but she led the creative process.

Step 2: Self-Disrupt and Identify Fakers

Early in my career as a PhD student, I attended a leadership conference at Harvard Business School. As you might imagine, I was drawn to the sessions on innovation management, so I attended one session where high-tech executives discussed the challenges they faced. One executive told the story about how the product she launched generated millions in revenues, well beyond the expected profits. I was intrigued, so I asked a question: "How do you know when the timing is right to launch your product?" She gave me a withering look and replied, "When your phone is ringing." Everyone in the audience laughed.

I felt foolish until I reminded myself that my question was one that scholars in my field had struggled with for decades. If the scholars had no answer yet, maybe this executive didn't either. Then I wondered something else: what would have happened if the executive had admitted, *I don't know*. Would she have seemed less confident, and so have lost her perceived leadership edge? Was she merely trying to protect her image as a leader?

Ask any person whether confidence is important for leadership, and they will tell you that of course it is. One leader said, "If you have a sinking ship, and your leader is paralyzed with fear, how is that person going to mobilize others to action to save lives? Instead, you want a leader who is calm and confident, to keep subordinates from utter panic."

This would seem to make a lot of intuitive sense, if confidence were a true reflection of competence. But what if the captain of the sinking ship was a faker? That is, what if you'd hired the captain because he sounded competent and seemed confident and capable, but in reality, he was faking it to get the job? Or, what if the captain was *so* confident in his knowledge that he is leery of trying something new when creative solutions are needed?

Is it easy to fake confidence? You bet. Just ask Amy Cuddy, whose brilliant work with Dana Carney and Andy Yap showed that posing like Wonder Woman for two minutes made participants feel more confident. Amy Cuddy's book, *Presence,* which has become a major bestseller, is based upon the theory that one can fake it until one makes it. And this solution is especially helpful for those of us who are competent but need that boost in self-confidence to help us on our way.

Be cautious, though — there can be a dark side to the power pose. There are some people who are not competent and really don't care about learning or improving; they just power pose to seem competent so they can dominate. To that end, what kind of leader do you want to hire? The one who is actually competent or the one who power posed in the bathroom before her interview to make you *think* she was competent?

Fakers — those with confidence but little care to improve their competence — are dangerous. Research shows that fakers are more likely to gain high-status positions even though they are less competent. And worse, if you elect a faker to a leadership role, your group's performance goes *down.* Good fakers can fool you easily, so don't let them.

How do you know if someone is a faker? Cameron Anderson and his colleagues have conducted research showing that over-confident people — fakers who were less competent than confident — speak first in a group, take up more air time, and are calm and relaxed. In contrast, people who are truly competent — those people you actually want to lead — don't behave in this way. Competent people speak up only when they have something to say. Fakers claim to know the answers, and they aren't humble, unless they believe that appearing so will make them look good.

What does a faker do in times of uncertainty when creativity is needed? In times of uncertainty, a faker will try and convince you that his answer is the best. He won't give you a range of possible solutions. He won't talk about the possibility of being wrong. He won't try to diagnose the problem by asking questions. He won't say *I don't know.* Fakers tend to veer away from admitting uncertainty or tolerating it because they know that admitting uncertainty to those with antiquated stereotypes of leadership could diminish the perception that they are leaderlike.

The good news is this: Taking credit for knowing the answers and having the best answer is a key trait of a faker, so be on the lookout for people who show no uncertainty. Be forewarned — leaders who show no uncertainty in their approach are often faking it.

Does this mean that you need to throw confidence out with the bathwater? No. I'm suggesting that you still look for confidence, but confidence of a different flavor. You can be confident and curious. You can be confident and not know the answer at the same time. Do you think Jada needed courage and confidence to question the direction of the group? You bet! She needed courage because she went against the group's direction, and also because she didn't have the answer to the question she asked.

Step 3: Learn to Recognize Creative Leadership

When looking for creative leadership, focus less on what people *say* about themselves and their ideas and more on the *actions* they engage in to shift the direction of the group. I'm not talking about promoting people who generate lots of creative ideas, although this does indicate flexible thinking. I'm not talking about promoting leaders who support employees generating lots of ideas — the traditional definition of a creative leader. Just like Procter and Gamble, CEOs can encourage creative-idea generation, but they can also promote rigorous stage-gate processes (like Bob McDonald did) and other practices that kill creative change. I'm talking about identifying those people who have a knack for understanding the creative process and who can help groups move forward when stuck. The essence of creative leadership is helping employees disrupt and embrace productive new directions.

One way to exhibit creative leadership is to ask questions. I'm not talking about the individual who questions everything. Asking questions simply for the sake of asking questions can disrupt group momentum and morale. I'm taking about identifying the person who understands when questions need to be asked. Creative leaders know to ask the right questions when groups show signs of poor decision making, or when problems emerge that need solving. There are also many instances when a group *needs* disrupting. Two of the most common occur when group members polarize in an extreme direction, and when group members conform in ways that block out creativity.

Creative Leaders Know When to Disrupt

Group polarization. If you look at the example of Jada, there were two key moments when she chose to ask her questions. The first was when the group polarized in an extreme direction. Group polarization happens when people jockey for status and end up taking a more and more extreme position regarding risk during decision making. What you saw in the group meeting is called a *conservative shift*. That is, the group shifted in an extremely conservative direction that valued low risk. You can see this conservative shift begin when Jim mentions feasibility concerns, which Tom escalates to bioterrorism, and Susan then escalates further to include a hacker war with China.

You can also have the opposite — a *risky shift* — occur when a group shifts toward endorsing ideas with extremely high risk. When groups polarize to an extreme position (a conservative or a risky shift), they definitely need disrupting. In the case of the meeting above, the group went dangerously close to choosing the status quo and doing nothing to solve the problem. Creative leaders usually have a finger on the pulse of groups and will recognize when they veer out of balance in their risk preferences. These leaders bring their groups back into balance by asking questions to disrupt and focus them.

Group conformity. Group conformity can take many shapes and sizes when groups decide which ideas to pursue and push to the next level. In general, group conformity becomes a problem when groups get stuck and bogged down. In my experience, when groups generate options, they can get stuck generating the same kind of solution. For example, Leigh Thompson at Northwestern University developed a brainstorming paradigm where people brainstorm different ways to clean up pet excrement. When I run this brainstorming task, I'll often see groups generate many different kinds of ideas with the same properties (e.g., different kinds of bags, including no-smell bags, no-rip bags, scented bags, easy-tear bags, etc.). When this happens, group members aren't adding as much value but are just iterating and conforming on the same basic kind of idea. So leadership in this context would involve a person recognizing that the group is anchored on the same kind of idea (in this case, bags), point this out, and then ask questions to shift the group in a new direction. (The leader might say, "All our solutions are for people walking their dogs. What about a busy mom who doesn't have time to walk her dog but has to clean the yard?")

When groups are selecting various ideas to pursue and face creative change, they can still conform and anchor. Groups can anchor when people start framing the selection decision in the same way. That is, members of groups can converge on using a how/best or even a why/potential way of viewing an idea. In the meeting example above, Rick starts vetting each idea, asking which one is best, and this problem frame is echoed by Tom, who describes his definition of the best idea. So this group is beginning to anchor its discussion in a how/best way of evaluating ideas.

When groups converge on a how/best problem frame to vet ideas, one of two things happens pretty quickly. They either choose a solution and move on to the next issue, or they get stuck. The how/best method is really efficient for making decisions fast. But if you want new or novel ideas, an uninterrupted how/best frame is likely to produce a more conservative shift. In this case, the goal of the creative leader is to ask a question to help shift the group away from a how/best problem frame. When the group above got stuck using their how/best problem frame, Jada disrupted them by asking a simple question that forced them to broaden and come up with options. She asked a brainstorming question, "How can we make this work?"

Creative Leaders Ask Questions

There are three kinds of questions my colleagues and I have identified as key to helping groups disrupt. Each kind of question solves a different problem that groups or even individuals can have when selecting creative ideas. When diagnosing creative leadership, look for people who know what to ask when.

Question 1: What problem are we trying to solve? Albert Einstein is believed to have said, "If I had sixty minutes to solve an important problem, I would spend fifty-five minutes on defining the problem and five minutes on the solution."

For the past fifteen years, I've run a simple simulation in my MBA classroom. I tell the students, who are in groups of four to five, to make a decision about how to solve a problem. I give the group a list of options to select from. If you assign each person in the group different preferences (as often happens spontaneously in groups), members immediately start negotiating and politicking to get their solution chosen. But it is a rare group that asks the simple question "What is the real problem we are trying to solve?" When they do, they make a better and more informed decision.

In my experience, teams of executives often tend to converge quickly on a how/best way of approaching problem solving. When this happens, they may *believe* that they understand the problem they are trying to solve. But when I look deeper, I routinely find that these teams have only a surface understanding of the problem.

They will say, "We want the company to be profitable," and quickly move on. But wanting to be profitable isn't actually a problem that needs solving, it's a goal. When you are identifying a problem that needs solving, you begin to understand tradeoffs and constraints. You can see Jim in the example above beginning to grapple with tradeoffs when he identifies the problem that needs solving: making a cost-effective decision while also improving patient healthcare. In other words, a creative leader doesn't just ask the question "What problem are we trying to solve?" and move on. A creative leader has a sense of whether members of the group really understand the problem and the tradeoffs and real constraints they face.

Creative leaders can also ask, "What problem are we trying to solve?" about the future. This is the magic of Marc Andreessen's role in the venture capital firm Andreessen Horowitz. When he asks about the future, he expands how the group is viewing the problem at hand by focusing them beyond the present constraints.

I believe that deeply understanding the problem you are trying to solve both in the present and in the future is the critical piece of leading the creative process. It is important when you lead idea-generation efforts and it is equally important when you lead efforts to select which ideas to pursue. Creative leaders have a sense of when groups are merely choosing solutions versus actually solving problems. Groups merely choose solutions when members politick and negotiate for their own self-interests. Groups solve problems when they identify solutions that manage the tradeoff they face. When creative leaders see that groups are just choosing solutions, they must have the confidence to halt the forward momentum and to redirect the group toward problem solving.

Question 2: Why does this solution have value? When Sarah Harvey at University College London and I examined decision-making teams, we identified that *why* questions helped teams embrace new ideas.

We found that teams would often converge on a solution, usually by using how/best ways of vetting the idea. When this happened, it was common for these solutions to be extremely feasible — which is important — but we also found that groups could sometimes choose ideas just because they knew their organization could easily achieve them. The problem, of course, is that just because an organization can do something doesn't mean their customers will buy it, or that it will solve problems.

The benefit of asking the *why* question is that it helps groups broaden, recalibrate, and see the larger picture. One team was ready to endorse an extremely feasible idea until a member asked, "Why does this idea help achieve our goals?" When the member asked this question, the team lost steam. Some members got annoyed because they enjoyed making progress. But then someone on the team admitted that the solution wasn't really in line with the company's broader strategic mission, nor did it solve the immediate problems they believed customers had. So in the end, this team made a good decision not to endorse an extremely feasible idea that probably would not have yielded profit.

Question 3: How can we make this solution work? When leaders ask, "How can we make this work?" they are using a type of broadening strategy within the FAB framework. What's nice about this kind of question is that my work with Scott Eidelman from the University of Arkansas shows that getting people to brainstorm before making decisions can help diminish their preference for the status quo. We are still nailing down the mechanisms, but my intuition is that brainstorming implies the status quo isn't that great and needs improvement. Brainstorming ideas also allows group members to have fun and feel good, and so diminishes any anxiety about making a bad or wrong decision.

Creative Leaders Strive for a Balance Between How/Best and Why/Potential Problem Frames

Creative leaders are in tune with the balance of how/best and why/potential ways of framing a problem. Generally, you want an equal balance. When groups veer too much in one direction the creative leader knows to start asking questions to get the group going in a more balanced direction. For example, although it is uncommon, I've seen groups that veer too far in the why/potential direction. One group was off in the weeds talking about the future implications of the idea, and the creative leader brought the group back into focus by simply asking, "How do we make this idea feasible *now*?"

Creative Leaders Understand
the Process of Inquiry

Think for a moment about some of the more accomplished creative leaders of our time: Dr. Tom Fogarty funds founders who understand the process of innovation. Mark Parker, CEO of Nike and named *Fortune*'s Businessperson of the Year in 2015, started his career as a designer. Parker used a process of experimentation to design, which he describes as "Conceptualizing, creating. Putting it on the athlete, getting all that feedback and then modifying. The whole process was a very tight loop."

Novo Nordisk CEO Lars Sorensen was chosen as the top CEO in the world in 2015 by Harvard Business School. He says that his leadership style in more recent years has become "involved with the research side." Larry Page, CEO of Google — and the top-rated CEO on Glassdoor — was experimenting from an early age, having built an inkjet printer out of Legos while getting his undergraduate degree at the University of Michigan. While pursuing a PhD in computer science, Page started a research project that was soon to become the focus of his dissertation — building what is now Google's search engine.

Creative leaders understand the process of inquiry, often because they have trained in it. One of the most powerful processes of inquiry that exists is the experimental method. Look at any discipline within the sciences and humanities and it will employ some version of the experimental method. In my experience, the experimental method isn't something that is brought into the MBA or undergrad business educational curriculum in any real way. MBAs don't do real research projects or write master's theses. If MBA or even undergraduate business students are exposed to research, statistics, experimental method, measurement, it's usually only at a surface level.

So, if you wish to cultivate more creative leadership in your organization, an easy place to start is by hiring candidates with meaningful research experience. Look for undergraduate and graduate students who have spent two or more years as research assistants in a professor's lab — the discipline doesn't matter. Look to see if these students have presented papers at conferences or published articles with their professors in journals with high impact factor (this is a measure of how many times the average journal article has been cited in a given year). If candidates have entrepreneurial experience, look to see whether they used some version of the experimental method (e.g., lean startup methodology) to achieve company results.

One key sign that candidates have had a meaningful research experience (as opposed to merely surface-level exposure to research) is to ask them specifically what questions they are curious about and the studies they have designed to explore them. Furthermore, during interviews, look to see if these candidates can use the experimental method to describe how they would approach solving a problem *you* care about. In other words, when choosing leaders, look to see whether candidates used a process to obtain results, rather than focusing only on their past experience or end results.

When choosing creative leaders, you are looking for people who have the skills to transform their curiosity into improving products and processes you can use. Knowing facts about accounting, finance, or even management is good, but it's not enough. Having experience working in an industry is also fine, but also not enough. You are looking for someone who has shown the initiative to gain the research skills beyond what is typically taught in the classroom. You are looking for someone who has had a real-world research experience and can use this process to solve problems your organization needs solved.

In sum, if we care about creative change, it is critical that we select leaders who can tolerate and manage the uncertainty of others. The first sign of a leader who can tolerate uncertainty is one who admits that she or he doesn't know the answer. I've seen some leaders exhibit this kind of uncertainty by saying, "We will find out the answer through a rigorous process of allowing it to emerge from our people."

And remember to retrain your brain to recognize creative leadership. If a person isn't yet a leader and says, "I don't know," the old-school approach might categorize this person as weak, or lacking competence. But that is backward thinking. Instead, re-categorize this kind of a statement as indicating that this person has the inner strength to be authentic and humble.

Once you retrain your brain to categorize those who admit that they don't know as being authentic and having leadership potential, then you can look to see what they *do* know that indicates creative leadership. Creative leaders might not know the end result now, but they do know the process to develop the answers you need.

8

Stop Generating Ideas and Start Making Impact

THE FIELD OF CREATIVITY ALWAYS RECOMMENDS generating more and more ideas. The more ideas you generate, the higher the likelihood that any one of them will be the smash success that fully makes an employee's career or makes a company millions.

Corporate America has certainly embraced this advice. Google is said to give 20 percent free time to employees to develop and explore ideas that meet with corporate priorities. More and more large companies are encouraging *intrapreneurship* — where employees are encouraged to design and to bring into being new ventures within their current companies. Crowdsourcing websites like Amazon's Mechanical Turk and P&G's Connect + Develop can, depending upon the complexity of the problem and the number of users on the platform, generate hundreds of ideas an hour. Research suggests that a good number of these ideas are of high quality.

But what do you think about this? In 2015, I sat in the audience at an innovation conference, listening to five corporate C-suite executives talk about the innovation challenges they faced. Each one of them was passionate about innovation and wanted more of it. I asked the group fairly pointedly, "Are you looking for *more* ideas?" Each person in turn emphatically said *no!* They all agreed that the challenge they faced was not about generating lots of alternatives. In his book *The Lean Startup,* Eric Ries notes that product development managers also have the same lament — they have plenty of ideas to choose from. Generating more solutions is not the issue.

Clearly, we have overcome the creative-idea-generation hurdle. Ideas are ten a penny. We stand atop all these ideas, looking down at our pile of creative concepts. But what I'm seeing are growing numbers of executives outwardly responding to this pile of ideas with disdain. Why are executives so down on new ideas?

Because they are becoming overwhelmed.

One company noted that a single day of employee-brainstorming time generated so many ideas that it took two months for management to review and discuss them, let alone actually take action on any. Executives were dumbfounded at how much time and effort they needed to manage the idea deluge from that single day.

Idea-generation programs create a huge workload increase for management, who are required to listen to, analyze, and consider myriad options from a flood of employee pitches. And what does increased time pressure to consider multiple options do to creative change? Studies have shown that as you increase the number of options a person has to consider, his preference for the status quo *increases.* As you increase decision makers' workloads, their preference for novel options decreases. In other words, generating lots of options and then adding workload pressure into the mix is a guaranteed recipe for executives rejecting creative change.

The problem, of course, is that creative idea generation efforts are occurring in organizations without the benefit of creative change efforts. Creative idea generation without a clear focus on making creative change overwhelms management and has the end result of leaving the very creative ideas you hoped to cultivate languishing in the file drawer.

But there is a silver lining. I wrote this book because I believe that we *can* engineer organizations for creative idea generation *and* creative change. That is, you *can* have both. To do so, we need to consider how to integrate both systems, as opposed to what we are doing now, which is to focus only on one. We need to build creative change into the very fabric of how we generate creative ideas.

CULTIVATING CREATIVE IDEA GENERATION
WITH CREATIVE CHANGE

For every skunk works you put in operation, every dollar you spend on R&D, every brainstorming training you give to your employees, and every crowdsourcing platform you use to generate the best new solution, you also need to make creative change within your organization for breakthrough ideas to have a real impact. I call this *the 1 to 1 ratio of creative idea generation to change.* For every hour, dollar, thought, and meeting spent on generating or developing a creative idea, spend the same time, effort, and money designing the organization and equipping your employees with skills to embrace it.

You cannot escape the reality that generating creative ideas is hard work, right? Well, there is an argument to be made that creative change is just as time-consuming and as resource-draining as generating the idea in the first place. So without carefully setting up a system to manage creative change in your organization, your attempts to capitalize on creative opportunity will fail.

And once you are willing to spend the time and effort to develop creative change, you can start to pinpoint the precise locations where your organization strangles and kills it. Every organization is different in terms of structure, people, and values when it comes to managing for creativity. So there is no one-size-fits-all way to implement creative change initiatives. However, one pattern I'm seeing is that companies and employees are quite *proactive* in how they plan their idea-generation efforts, but quite *reactive* in how they plan for creative change. One of the more typical scenarios I see in large organizations is the following:

Lisa is a marketing executive at a large consumer-products company. She was excited when everyone in her department agreed that the idea she proposed, while needing some tweaking, was terrific. After Lisa suggested the idea, the group came together, refined it, and put together a prototype. It worked. Consumers said they loved it.

The entire process had taken six months of hard work, and time was of the essence. After Lisa received buy-in from her department head, her group decided they could launch the product relatively quickly. They committed to a launch date. All she needed now was the approval of a few more people from the regulatory department, and then a couple of people in upper management. That shouldn't be too hard, right?

Thinking it was going to be a slam dunk, Lisa decided to send Regulatory a copy of the prototype for review. When she received their feedback, she was stunned. They recommended tabling it.

Lisa quickly set up a meeting with Dave, the head of Regulatory. At the meeting, she told Dave that her entire department and division stood behind this project, and it had tested beautifully with consumers. She told him that the CEO was mandating more innovation, and her group was working hard to answer that call.

Dave patiently listened to all Lisa's impassioned pleas, and said, "This has the potential to create a huge lawsuit for us. We just can't give this a thumbs-up."

Lisa couldn't believe her ears. She went back to tell her team, and they were understandably incensed. They complained that Regulatory was totally biased against anything new. Regulatory were the bad guys, they all said. The team felt that it didn't matter how much they improved their idea, Regulatory would always say no, no matter what. Everyone agreed that they needed backing from Regulatory before making the pitch to upper management, but they also agreed that Regulatory had no incentive to say yes. In the end, the team lost steam, they tabled the project, and the group's numbers started to fall.

Whose fault is it that Lisa's project failed? Was Regulatory the cause? Or did Lisa and her team cause the problem? The executives of the company where this event happened wanted to know who was to blame. Everyone wanted to point the finger. The problem never got fixed because nobody knew the answer. What if no one was to blame? What if the cause of the problem was multidimensional and rooted in how Lisa, the team, and the organization approached creative change?

Cultivating Proactive Creative Change versus Reactive Creativity Rejection

Analyzing this scenario at the three different levels — Lisa (i.e., the individual employee), the team, and the organization — can provide a snapshot into how *you* can diagnose where creative change initiatives fail in *your* organization. Once you know where the bottlenecks and dead ends are, you can learn how to design a system to prevent them from happening. And I believe you can design these systems even if you aren't a decision maker and have no formal authority.

Let's take a look at how Lisa managed creative change. Lisa was quite successful on two fronts. She made creative change with her team and her boss. But why couldn't she make creative change with Dave? There are four pitfalls that I think hold people back from addressing creative change until it is too late.

The first pitfall is one I regularly experience myself. In the course of generating our ideas, we can fall madly in love with them. We can build the case in our own minds that each of these ideas is terrific as-is, and that one's colleagues are being shortsighted or biased against creativity if they reject them. So we can instantly resist feedback — especially when it is negative — even though this kind of feedback can be the most valuable to helping us hone our ideas. Notice Lisa and her team's reaction to Dave's feedback. The team didn't immediately go about fixing the problem Dave unearthed, which might have been an easy fix. They were just too busy being angry and pointing fingers.

The second pitfall is the instinct to improve and to refine our ideas to the point where they are polished before we are willing to share them with others. Like Lisa, people may believe that the right time to make creative change for outsiders (e.g., Dave) is when the project is finished — and thus perfected. Lisa waited until the idea was, in her mind, finalized before she approached Dave. This, of course, set up an unrealistic expectation.

I also see the opposite — employees who brainstorm several undeveloped ideas with decision makers to see which ones decision makers like the most. This strategy also tends to backfire. My work shows that decision makers view employees who brainstorm numerous ideas with them (versus selling one idea to them at a time, or asking them for feedback about one idea) as relatively unfocused, inefficient, and naive. Brainstorming many ideas with decision makers (as opposed to asking for feedback to refine a single idea) is more likely to overwhelm rather than impress one's bosses.

The third related pitfall is that when generating and refining an idea, we can forget that there are many users of our idea. The customers who will use your product are only one kind of user. Management also has to use your product, in the sense that they have to buy into it. So while it is common to test our ideas and gain feedback from customers or consumers, we tend not to gain feedback from others inside the organization — including decision makers — early during the idea-generation process.

The fourth pitfall is that it is easy to use the wrong strategy when trying to enact creative change. Lisa uses a straight-up selling strategy when approaching Dave. Lisa sells her idea like she might share a familiar idea — she notes enthusiastically that lots of people like it.

But creative ideas are tricky for experts, because it can be difficult to see their distinct usefulness. And every decision maker's view of usefulness might be different. In the case of Dave, he didn't really care if lots of customers liked the idea. He simply cared if the idea was legal. Lisa could have used an analogy to compare the legality of her idea to another idea already legally in use somewhere else, for example. But she didn't take that step.

To make matters slightly more complicated, our instinct to hold on to our ideas and to shield them from view can have important benefits. For one, we already know that a managers' typical knee-jerk reaction is to dislike new ideas. If we share our ideas with others and they dislike them, our ideas might get bad press within the organization before they even have a chance to show benefits.

Getting feedback from outsiders can also harm an idea's creativity. Clayton Christensen of Harvard Business School said: "You're not into it two weeks before you hear from sales or finance or engineering that they will block it unless you change it to fit their needs. These powerful constituencies inside the company collectively beat things into a shape that more closely conforms to the existing business model rather than to the opportunity in the market."

In other words, when it comes to making creative change, you have some serious barriers to overcome. And people are more likely to resist and to dislike your creative ideas if they are external decision makers with a how/best view. So stalling and leaving creative change to the last minute will almost certainly fail.

Begin the idea-generation process with creative change fully in mind. The way to step around these pitfalls is to build creative change into the way that you generate the idea in the first place. Christensen's concern about internal pork-barrel politics harming your idea's distinctiveness is a real concern. The good news is that these kinds of concerns can be managed, but not on the fly.

Concerns from inside (or outside) your organization can be managed using the FAB (fit, aha, broaden) framework described in Chapter 5. You can alter the product or idea so that it addresses the concern by employing the feedback pitch, for example. Alternatively, you can decide not to change the idea itself at all. Instead, you can frame your idea as already addressing this concern (without actually changing the idea itself), for example, by using a variety of fit (the cues you use to describe your idea) or aha (combination) strategies. This latter method is less about developing the idea in question and more about refining how you communicate your creative idea to others.

In other words, you don't always have to change the idea itself to deal with decision makers' concerns. If you are worried that changing an idea will diminish its distinct value, then you can choose merely to change the way to frame and communicate the idea to decision makers. If you can modify the original idea in a way that does not destroy its distinct use, then you can use this fact to gain decision makers' buy-in after implementing their suggestions.

If you are concerned that a decision maker's feedback will harm the quality of your idea, you could gather data to verify whether your concerns were valid. For example, you could have two separate groups of customers provide feedback on two versions of the same prototype — one adapted to address a decision maker's feedback, and one not. You can actually test to see whether decision makers are helping or hurting an idea's appeal. But this, of course, takes a great deal of time and planning to enact.

Had Lisa approached Dave at a much earlier stage with her idea, she could have received feedback before she had committed to a product launch. Then her team could decide whether or not the feedback would harm the distinctiveness and value of the idea. If the solution the team generated to address Dave's feedback made the idea better, this would obviously be great news. Lisa could then set up a second meeting with Dave, thank him for his feedback, and ask for his approval after showing him how her team had addressed his concerns.

And if the solution they generated actually harmed the value of the idea, this is actually also good news. First, they'd have data to show that it decreased the value of the idea. Second, they will now know they need to change how they're framing the idea for Dave. The team's goal is to appeal to Dave's interests, and because they now know what those interests are, they're in a better position to do so.

You can frame the same idea very differently for different kinds of decision makers. Jane Howell, at Ivey Business School at the University of Western Ontario, describes advice from one successful idea champion who suggested that selling an idea requires a person to "understand what people need to hear and give them the information in the form that they can process in a way that is useful for them." Howell gives the example of an employee in an automobile-manufacturing company who sells his idea to replace the current automobile airbags utilized by his company — which are now priced at $75 each — with a much less expensive version that will be priced at only $5 each. "You tell the president of the company, who has a marketing background, that there are 50 million cars, each with an airbag, currently using a $75 solution and we now have a $5 solution. You tell the guy who is running manufacturing that he won't have to buy any capital equipment to do this job." The point is that the president of the company might care about cost, while the manufacturing decision maker might care about safety and feasibility. To effectively sell an idea, you need to pitch it as addressing each decision maker's specific concern.

In other words, ideas succeed in organizations only if they are seen by executives as fitting the company's unique ecosystem. The sales pitch described by Jane Howell is an example of a pitch where you frame the idea as already fitting with a decision maker's interests. For this strategy to work, it is imperative that you know precisely at the start of the process what the decision maker's interests truly are.

Here's the bottom line: Will a new idea perfectly fit each group's unique concerns? Probably not. Will other groups be resistant to your ideas? Highly likely! Are there other strategies Lisa could have used to successfully make creative change with Dave and others? Absolutely!

When managing creative change, the picture gets complicated quickly. Every situation where you attempt to make creative change will be different because the players will likely be different. Instead of reacting to the situation as it unfolds, I recommend planning and strategizing to proactively manage the process of making creative change. You need to start thinking about creative change the moment you and your team embrace a new solution to pursue.

When you begin the process of generating and developing your ideas, do it with creative change in mind. And don't try to do all of this yourself — enlist the help of others whenever possible.

The Power of Change Circles. Some companies — like Google — inherently know the value of change circles, getting small groups of people together with the common purpose of making change. In 2012, Megan Smith was vice president of X (at that time called Google X). She recognized that women in technology were getting relatively little credit for their contributions. So she started Women Techmakers, a program where Google gives employees free time to discuss how to increase visibility and resources for women in technology. Part of the benefit is creating a network of people united by a common cause. But there is a second benefit of thinking through how to sell and pitch ideas with others in the room who can give you feedback and disrupt your ineffective habits when selling a creative idea.

When I lead seminars on creative change, I ask executives in the audience this question: "How many of you have had creative ideas you could not get others in your company to endorse?" Most people raise their hands in response. I then put people in groups — change circles — and have them use FAB to start brainstorming different approaches to frame and sell their ideas.

I've started to notice patterns. The first pattern is that executives start sharing their ideas, usually by saying, "I've tried everything, but . . ." I also hear statements like "Management is just biased against creativity . . ."

I've learned that people can get stuck in and limited by a losing sales pitch or pessimistic beliefs. Just like you can get stuck when trying to solve a problem creatively and can't find the answer, you can get stuck when trying to sell an idea and you don't know the correct framing. One of the most effective ways to break out of your dilemma is to solicit help from others.

The second pattern I tend to notice is that those presenting their ideas to the group are often surprised at how many enlightening ways meeting members respond to them. Sometimes I'll even hear meeting members ask great questions like "How is telling the CEO that our business will fail in ten years going to make her feel the failure now?" In other words, you can try and use FAB on your own, but a better approach is to find others whom you trust and bounce your ideas off them first.

So who should you recruit to solicit for this kind of feedback in a change circle meeting? People from different departments. Adding diversity of perspectives to your change circle will only enhance its value. Had Lisa formed a change circle right at the start of her project, she might have learned that people need Regulatory's approval for projects early on in the process. Others in the organization are likely to have had the same encounter Lisa had, and she could have benefited from their experience.

Further, you might even invite people from departments where, at some point, you're going to need approval. You can find out who knows the decision makers in question, and which decision makers are more resistant to change, versus those who are open to new ideas. In other words, you can gain allies from other departments in your quest to make the change you desire.

If you care about making change in your organization, creative or otherwise, starting a change circle will be a rewarding experience. Change circles can meet as often as you like, but I recommend weekly meetings. I also recommend that change circles include about five people. There's a reason for this. Naturally occurring discussion groups tend to tap out at around five people. More than five people means that someone won't get air time during your discussions. Some change circles will begin with a particular problem or challenge that a member of the circle is facing and end with suggestions and updates from the other members. I find that most members can spend up to an hour thinking through a single change initiative, so plan to discuss one change issue per meeting.

There are many variations of the creative-change strategies I've included in this book. One employee shared her take on her feedback pitch, where she asked a decision maker in passing, "My team has been kicking around this idea. What do you think?" She noticed that giving a feedback pitch very early on in a project started a very different conversation than waiting till later in the process and only then saying, "My team has been working day and night on this project for months. What do you think?"

In the former case, she received key information about what this decision maker thought early enough in the process to know exactly how to pitch the idea to this same person later. And she found that the decision maker didn't even remember the conversation, but he loved the fact that her pitch later on was so clearly related to his interests. In the latter case, the decision maker was much more tentative about giving informal feedback and suggested setting a formal meeting time to document any decision. The latter approach made it much more difficult to learn what that decision maker might have actually wanted.

As you encounter change initiatives, I encourage you to send me your stories via my website, jennifersmueller.com. I'll do my best to post them on my blog page (I will mask your identity for confidentiality if you wish) and share them with others so we can all learn different ways of making creative change.

Coordinated Creative Change in Teams. Can one person lead the idea-generation process, champion the idea externally, and then manage the forward momentum of the project? Work by Ella Miron-Spektor and her colleagues suggests that the answer is often no. The process of generating ideas and then adapting the ideas to the organization is incredibly time-consuming and complex. It's easy to veer off too far in one direction, making the idea new or, in the other direction, making the idea feasible. There is even evidence that some people are really talented at one activity (e.g., developing ideas) but not necessarily the other (e.g., organizational politics). But teams that assign people either to generate ideas or to try and sell them externally can perform more effectively.

The solution in Chapter 6 of assigning two main decision makers partially solves this problem. If Lisa had adopted this approach, she might have assigned herself as the creative director of the team but assigned someone else — perhaps another manager — as the producer or budget manager, whose job it would have been to act as ambassador to all other groups.

In this case, the producer's job is — out of the gate — to set up meetings with all those external decision makers throughout the organization to better understand their needs and concerns. Then, while the team is designing the overall idea, the ambassador is busy negotiating externally, but also internally with the rest of the team as the idea develops. Dave's legal concerns would have been rooted out by a producer much earlier — perhaps at the very start of the idea-generation process.

Cross-functional teams sometimes assign ambassadors to each functional arm of a company. One company I worked with assigned their product engineer to interface with R&D, their marketing person to interface with marketing, and their operations person to interface with the main decision makers (who happened to have a background in operations). The point is, creative change has a better shot of succeeding if your team assigns and distributes various external-relations roles throughout the idea-generation process.

Structuring Creative Change in Organizations. Most of the time, the decision makers are the highest-paid people in the room. In small companies, creative change may be easier to engineer because there are fewer of these kinds of people. The fewer people you have who need to say yes to an idea to make it fly, the less time it can take to gain internal buy-in. Of course, you also have a big problem in small companies if your only decision maker says no. In contrast, in a large company, you need lots of people to sign off on any idea, so the idea might die an early death at any of several approval stages. But you might also find managers in other parts of the organization who will say yes.

Many organizations are structured like fiefdoms, with each department controlling one piece of the decision-making pie. This means that decision making for innovation can involve one group of upper-level managers who make the up-or-out decision. But, along the way, those who are championing new ideas need to sell to *all* the fiefdoms to get their ideas through. In Lisa's case, the decision to go forward needed a green light from three layers — the team leader, the Regulatory department, and the upper management decision-making body. So decision making in that case was decentralized and hierarchical, a structure that can make things difficult for creative teams to get their ideas accepted.

In contrast, if your CEO or main decision maker is involved in the process of idea generation with you, you are in luck — that person will have an easier time buying into the idea. If your main decision maker has an inventor's mindset, you are also in luck. Those leading Google's version of a skunk works, X, have an open line to Sergey Brin and Larry Page, Google's cofounders, who think like inventors and interpret failure as merely a step toward progress. So showing them the flaws won't necessarily stall a project.

However, in the example above, Dave was a lone decision maker who viewed his role as purely evaluative. He wasn't in a problem-solving mode, saying "How can we make this work?" He simply said no. This is not a function of who Dave is or of his personality, but of the way Dave's role is structured. Dave's role is head of Regulatory, and he was just doing his job — he was regulating.

So how organizations structure their decision-making roles can shift the strategies you use and the amount of time you need to spend to manage creative change. The more decision-making layers there are, the more time and effort it will take for you to manage them. The fewer the layers, the more easily you might integrate decision makers more directly into the idea-generation process.

If you are leading an organization, it's key that you learn how many layers of decision making your employees need to go through to make creative change. If you have more than one layer of formal decision-making authority, chances are the most creative ideas that are trying to bubble up in your company are dying an early death.

I'm never surprised when CEOs of large organizations tell me, "I don't understand why my people aren't generating creative ideas." Usually I find out that they are — it's just that their ideas are being killed by all the bureaucratic decision-making layers. Once you know the number of layers and who the decision makers are, then you can start redesigning the system with checks — but also balances. You might also decide to trim the layers of decision makers. If your decision makers use the self-disruption strategies outlined in Chapter 4, my bet is that you will need only one layer — and remember, you can use the wisdom-of-crowds method to winnow the ideas you present down to a reasonable number.

WHY CREATIVE CHANGE IS HERE TO STAY

When you generate lots of ideas, you can overwhelm people, and creative change may come to a standstill. This is the problem with only generating ideas. In reality, making creative change happen requires — in near-equal measure — idea generation, working within a creative-change process to manage the ideas that emerge, and then deciding to implement the ideas that show greatest promise. And the work around creative change never really ends. Our resistance to creative ideas isn't going away — ever. The reason is that once a creative idea is adopted, used, implemented, and institutionalized, it becomes the status quo.

The big-picture, take-home message for you is this: We have been managing creativity like it is a rational process of assessing risk, instead of as a psychological process of managing uncertainty. When you treat a creative idea with this rational economic how/ best perspective, the uncertainty it poses for you is only a nuisance. From a how/best perspective, any idea that is uncertain becomes inefficient to pursue. From a how/best mindset, the only *great* ideas are those that we know with total certainty will work. And of course, when we define and limit *great* in this way, we exclude creative ideas and find ourselves highly prone to pursuing ideas that continue to fail with consumers and keep us stuck in the same downward loop toward irrelevance.

In other words, too many executives have bought into a very seductive lie. Executives want the world to be a predictable place, where people make good decisions because they are expert geniuses and make bad decisions because they just aren't that smart. Some decision making can work this way, but in truth, it doesn't work like this with creative change.

You can't assess the risk of a creative idea succeeding. It's not because you aren't smart and capable — it's because no one can know. The wisdom of crowds might tell you that lots of consumers like an idea, but it can't tell you if the technology for that idea is available and makes it feasible, if the idea has staying power, if market conditions will remain the same, or if another disruptive technology will come along to make your idea obsolete.

But once we accept that our metrics are not themselves the answers but rather that they are the *path* to the answers, we are no longer limited by fear. Now we can make some real choices. We can stop wasting our time trying to know the unknowable. Instead of avoiding anxiety and uncertainty, we can embrace them, because we can interpret the uncertainty as hope and attack it with a desire for discovery and real progress.

So be honest with yourself about whether you approach creativity with a how/best view. If you do, and you still want creative change, it's time to self-disrupt. But expect the disruption process to feel uncomfortable. Barry Staw, one of the most influential scholars in the field of management, observes: "Few managers want to pay the price for innovation. To most managers, being innovative means that they have to do *everything wrong.*"

Right now, managers don't know how to perform their role without feeling like they are doing everything wrong when it comes to creativity. But there is another way — one that helps managers feel like they are part of the process of invention rather than alienated by it. I've tried to outline what this other approach is and how to implement it. The strategies outlined in this book are intended to help lift ourselves and others to a place of balance: a skeptical kind of love rather than extreme love or hate.

And the best news of all is that people love creativity. When people perceive that an idea is creative, it makes them feel joyful and surprised. As long as we love creativity, we have the capacity to embrace creative ideas and change the status quo.

While the Science and Security Board of the *Bulletin of the Atomic Scientists* may have declared that the human race is just three minutes away from oblivion, I personally take a more hopeful view. For me, the fact that people have been managing creative idea generation without proactively managing creative change has a huge upside. Right now we are seeing the most pessimistic outcome ever for creativity — the routine rejection of creative ideas. We can't do any worse on the creative-change front than we are currently doing, so the only place to go is up.

But first we have to come to grips with the harsh reality that perhaps the biggest barrier to accepting new and fresh ideas comes from within ourselves. And the sooner we learn how to spot our unconscious resistance patterns and cope with them, the sooner we will start to make real and meaningful progress — and the sooner we can begin working together to embrace the world we want to live in.

Acknowledgments

There are too many people I want to thank. So I'm not going to thank everyone who deserves thanks here — I'll reserve that for many in-person thank-yous.

Instead, I want to focus only on those people who have directly contributed to this book. I want to start by thanking *you,* dear reader. Thank you for coming with me on this journey. You and I know how hard it is to make creativity work — and we both know it's a complicated and messy process. But you stuck with me, and you read this book (even my acknowledgments, it appears), and I appreciate your support and interest. I wrote this book for the person who truly wants more creativity in the world and aims to champion change. So if you are that person, I wrote this book for you. Please visit my website, jennifersmueller.com, or drop me a line or a comment via email so we can keep the dialogue going and help each other.

And then there are the people without whom this book would not exist. And I'm not just talking about my mom, with her wonderful illustration in Chapter 1 and her warm encouragement, or my dad, who inspired me to be a scientist in the first place; I'm talking about the people who literally told me that this was the book I was going to write. If you are reading this book and liked it, you should thank them too. I want to thank Giles Anderson, my agent, for pushing this book forward. And, of course, Rick Wolff, my editor at Houghton, who had the vision that made this book a reality. Rick rejected my first proposal, and my second, and said, "Jen, nobody wants to read a book from some researcher. You need to make these stories relatable and come to life." And he pushed me to do that. I also want to thank Peter Economy for helping improve my writing and encouraging me to make this book more cogent (and shorter).

Many of the ideas in this book were directly shaped by conversation and collaborations with Matthew Cronin and Jeffrey Loewenstein, whose insights and passion for the subject continue to inspire me.

In addition, to my research coauthors and collaborators, for the work I built upon to write this book, you deserve my heartfelt thanks: Teresa Amabile, Jack Goncalo, Shimul Melwani, Jennifer Deal, Sarah Harvey, Dishan Kamdar, Ethan Burris, Julia Minson, Rick Larrick, Vish Krishnan, Cheryl Wakslak, Jennifer Overbeck, Sigal Barsade, Scott Eidelman, Barry Staw, Priya Kannan-Narasimhan, and Mandy O'Neil.

I would also like to thank those who contributed to interviews and examples in the book, namely Thomas Fogarty, Jeffrey Solomon, Rob Cook, Rob B. McClary, Andrea Matwyshyn, Jenna Vondrasek, Austin Jacobs, Annie Ngo, Sean Wilson, Tim Cushanick, and Daniella Lisle.

Of course, where would I be without the person who inspired creative change for me — Steven Bengis — my husband, to whom I've dedicated this book. Thank you to my immediate family, Juliet, Kevin, Julia, Chet, Jonah, Ava, Ann, Cliff, Elke, Jeffrey, and Pete, for cheering me forward. And then there are the dogs — Butchy and Sammy — whom I thank for snuggling me throughout the writing process.

Now, let's go make some creative change.

Notes

Preface: The Seeds of Our Uncreative Destruction

page

x *the divine):* W. Niu and R. J. Sternberg, "The philosophical roots of Western and Eastern conceptions of creativity," *Journal of Theoretical and Philosophical Psychology* 26, no. 1–2 (2006): 18.

xi *than to embrace it:* B. M. Staw, "Why No One Really Wants Creativity," in *Creative Action in Organizations: Ivory Tower Visions and Real World Voices,* C. Ford, D. A. Gioia, eds. (Thousand Oaks, CA: Sage Publications, 1995).

old markets: J. Schumpeter, *Capitalism, Socialism, and Democracy* (New York: Harper & Brothers, 1942).

1. The Hidden Innovation Barrier

6 *most people chose:* D. Ellsberg, "Risk, Ambiguity, and the Savage Axioms," *Quarterly Journal of Economics* 75, no. 4 (1961): 643–669.

Ellsberg paradox: C. R. Fox and A. Tversky, "Ambiguity Aversion and Comparative Ignorance," *Quarterly Journal of Economics* 110, no. 3 (1995): 585–603.

7 *associated with creative ideas:* G. Day, "Is It Real? Can We Win? Is It Worth Doing?: Managing Risk and Reward in an Innovation Portfolio," *Harvard Business Review* 85, no. 12 (2007): 110.

9 *idea implementation:* R. M. Kanter, "When a Thousand Flowers Bloom: Structural, Collective, and Social Conditions for Innova-

tion in Organizations," in *Research in Organizational Behavior,* B. Staw and L. L. Cummings, eds. (Greenwich, CT: JAI Press, 1988).

13 *the status quo:* W. Samuelson and R. Zeckhauser, "Status Quo Bias in Decision Making," *Journal of Risk and Uncertainty* 1, no. 1 (1988): 7–59.

we think it is: D. Kahneman, J. L. Knetsch, and R. H. Thaler, "Anomalies: The Endowment Effect, Loss Aversion, and Status Quo Bias," *Journal of Economic Perspectives* 5, no. 1 (1991): 193–206.

14 *to avoid uncertainty:* L. Festinger, "A Theory of Social Comparison Processes," *Human Relations* 7, no. 2 (1954): 117–140; Charles R. Berger, "Uncertain Outcome Values in Predicted Relationships: Uncertainty Reduction Theory Then and Now," *Human Communication Research* 13, no. 1 (1986): 34–38; and M. A. Hogg and B. A. Mullin, "Uncertainty: Subjective Uncertainty Reduction and Group Identification," *Social Identity and Social Cognition* (1999): 249–279.

generate them: M. A. Cronin and J. Loewenstein, *The Craft of Creativity* (in development, Stanford University Press).

17 *lose its meaning:* L. Kwoh, "You Call That Innovation?," *Wall Street Journal,* May 23, 2012, www.wsj.com/articles/SB10001424052702304791704577418250902309914.

with the competitors: C. M. Christensen, M. E. Raynor, and R. Mc-Donald, "What Is Disruptive Innovation?," *Harvard Business Review,* December 2015.

22 *you can't know:* D. K. Simonton, "Scientific Creativity as Constrained Stochastic Behavior: The Integration of Product, Person, and Process Perspectives," *Psychological Bulletin* 4, no. 129 (2003): 475–494.

2. Our Love-Hate Relationship with Creativity

23 *human progress:* B. A. Hennessey and T. M. Amabile, "Creativity," *Annual Review of Psychology* 61 (2010): 569–598.

competitive advantage: R. W. Woodman, J. E. Sawyer, and R. W. Griffin, "Toward a Theory of Organizational Creativity," *Academy of Management Review* 18 (1993): 293–321.

scientific discovery: D. K. Simonton, *Origins of Genius: Darwin-*

ian Perspectives on Creativity. New York: Oxford University Press (1999): 308.

you guessed it, creativity: F. Kern, "What Chief Executives Really Want," *Bloomberg Businessweek,* May 17, 2010, www.bloomberg .com/news/articles/2010-05-18/what-chief-executives-really-want.

24 *"worship creativity":* D. Thompson, "Why Experts Reject Creativity," *The Atlantic,* October, 2014, www.theatlantic.com/business /archive/2014/10/why-new-ideas-fail/381275/.

to buy products: J. S. Mueller, J. Loewenstein, and J. Deal, "Managers Reject Ideas Customers Want," *Harvard Business Review,* July–August 2014, https://hbr.org/2014/07/managers-reject-ideas -customers-want.

the workplace: M. Baer, "Putting Creativity to Work: The Implementation of Creative Ideas in Organizations," *Academy of Management Journal* 55 (2012): 1102–1119; and E. F. Rietzschel, B. A. Nijstad, and W. Stroebe, "The Selection of Creative Ideas after Individual Idea Generation: Choosing between Creativity and Impact," *British Journal of Psychology* 101 (2010): 47–68.

school: E. L. Westby and V. L. Dawson, "Creativity: Asset or Burden in the Classroom?," *Creativity Research Journal* 8 (1995): 1–10.

academia: K. J. Boudreau, E. C. Guinan, K. R. Lakhani, and C. Riedl, "The Novelty Paradox & Bias for Normal Science: Evidence from Randomized Medical Grant Proposal Evaluations" (working paper, Harvard Business School, 2012).

sciences: K. Siler, K. Lee, and L. Bero, "Measuring the Effectiveness of Scientific Gatekeeping," *Proceedings of the National Academy of Sciences* 112 (2015): 360–365.

government: R. Fernandez and D. Rodrik, "Resistance to Reform: Status Quo Bias in the Presence of Individual-Specific Uncertainty," *American Economic Review* (1991): 1146–1155.

our personal lives: J. S. Mueller, S. Melwani, and J. A. Goncalo, "The Bias against Creativity: Why People Desire but Reject Creative Ideas," *Psychological Science* 23 (2012): 13–17; and C. P. Moreau and D. W. Dahl, "Designing the Solution: The Impact of Constraints on Consumers' Creativity," *Journal of Consumer Research* 32 (2005): 13–22.

26 *market hierarchies:* C. Christensen, *The Innovator's Dilemma: When New Technologies Cause Great Firms to Fail* (Boston: Harvard Business School Press, 2013).

27   *the iPhone:* J. Loewenstein and J. S. Mueller, "Implicit Theories of Creative Ideas: How Culture Shapes Assessments of Creative Ideas," *Academy of Management Discoveries* (forthcoming).

31   *a practical one:* J. S. Mueller, C. J. Wakslak, and V. Krishnan, "Construing Creativity: The How and Why of Recognizing Creative Ideas," *Journal of Experimental Social Psychology* 51 (2014): 81–87.

33   *group of people:* A. G. Greenwald and M. R. Banaji, "Implicit Social Cognition: Attitudes, Self-Esteem, and Stereotypes," *Psychological Review* 102 (1995): 4–27.

35   *sell a new idea:* G. Yukl, H. Kim, and C. Chavez, "Task Importance, Feasibility, and Agent Influence Behavior as Determinants of Target Commitment," *Journal of Applied Psychology* 84 (1999): 137–143; and R. B. Cialdini and N. J. Goldstein, "Social Influence: Compliance and Conformity," *Annual Review of Psychology* 55 (2004): 591–621.

36   *PillCam, a camera:* www.givenimaging.com/en-us/Innovative-Solutions/Capsule-Endoscopy/pillcam-colon/Pages/default.aspx.

3. The Science Behind the Paradox

49   *naive or misguided:* R. Sutton, "Why Creativity and Innovation Suck," on *Bob Sutton Work Matters,* December 1, 2007, http://bobsutton.typepad.com/my_weblog/2007/12/why-creativity.html.

52   *evaluating a creative idea:* M. D. Mumford, D. C. Lonergan, and G. Scott, "Evaluating Creative Ideas: Processes, Standards, and Context," *Inquiry: Critical Thinking Across the Disciplines* 22 (2002): 21–30; and T. M. Amabile, "Social Psychology of Creativity: A Consensual Assessment Technique," *Journal of Personality and Social Psychology* 43 (1982): 997–1013.

53   *novelty and impact:* K. Siler, K. Lee, and L. Bero, "Measuring the Effectiveness of Scientific Gatekeeping," *Proceedings of the National Academy of Sciences* 112 (2015): 360–365.

    of high quality: K. J. Boudreau, E. C. Guinan, K. R. Lakhani, and C. Riedl, "The Novelty Paradox & Bias for Normal Science: Evidence from Randomized Medical Grant Proposal Evaluations" (working paper, Harvard Business School, 2012), https://dash.harvard.edu/bitstream/handle/1/10001229/13-053.pdf?sequence=1.

company's website: L. J. Kornish and K. T. Ulrich, "The Importance of the Raw Idea in Innovation: Testing the Sow's Ear Hypothesis," *Journal of Marketing Research* 51 (2014): 14–26.

54 *thirty experts:* N. Escoffier and B. McKelvey, "The Wisdom of Crowds in the Movie Industry: Towards New Solutions to Reduce Uncertainties," *International Journal of Arts Management* 17 (2015): 52–63.

relative to novices: P. C. Moreau, D. R. Lehmann, and A. B. Markman, "Entrenched Knowledge Structures and Consumer Response to New Products," *Journal of Marketing Research,* 38, no. 1 (2001): 14–29.

level of experience: D. A. Shepherd, A. Zacharakis, and R. A. Baron, "VCs' Decision Processes: Evidence Suggesting More Experience May Not Always Be Better," *Journal of Business Venturing* 18 (2003): 381–401.

successful in the long term: L. Huang and J. L. Pearce, "Managing the Unknowable: The Effectiveness of Early-Stage Investor Gut Feel in Entrepreneurial Investment Decisions," *Administrative Science Quarterly* 60 (2015): 634–670.

55 *going to be useful:* B. A. Hennessey, T. M. Amabile, and J. S. Mueller, "Consensual Assessment," in *Encyclopedia of Creativity,* 2nd ed., M. A. Runco and S. R. Pritzker, eds. (San Diego, CA: Academic Press, 2011): 253–260.

with this view: P. Thiel, *Zero to One: Notes on Startups, or How to Build the Future* (New York: Crown Publishing Group, 2014).

56 *existing ideas:* T. B. Ward, "What's Old about New Ideas?," in *The Creative Cognition Approach,* S. M. Smith, T. B. Ward, R. A. Fiske, eds. (Cambridge, MA: MIT Press, 1995).

57 *devalue creative ideas:* T. M. Amabile, "Brilliant but Cruel: Perceptions of Negative Evaluators," *Journal of Experimental Social Psychology* 19 (1983): 146–156.

58 *color swatches:* C. Martindale and K. Moore, "Priming, Prototypicality, and Preference," *Journal of Experimental Psychology: Human Perception and Performance* 14, 661 (1988).

paintings: P. Hekkert and P. Wieringen, "Complexity and Prototypicality as Determinants of the Appraisal of Cubist Paintings," *British Journal of Psychology* 81 (1990): 483–495.

and music: J. D. Smith and R. J. Melara, "Aesthetic Preference and Syntactic Prototypicality in Music: 'Tis the Gift to be Simple," *Cognition* 34, no. 3 (1990): 279–298.

views of creativity: W. Niu and R. J. Sternberg, "Cultural Influences on Artistic Creativity and Its Evaluation," *International Journal of Psychology* 36 (2001): 225–241.

59 *inspired them with awe:* J. Loewenstein and J. S. Mueller, "Implicit Theories of Creative Ideas: How Culture Shapes Assessments of Creative Ideas," *Academy of Management Discoveries* (forthcoming).

select the idea too: F. J. Flynn and J. A. Chatman, "Strong Cultures and Innovation: Oxymoron or Opportunity?," in *International Handbook of Organizational Culture and Climate,* C. L. Cooper, S. Cartwright, and P. C. Earley, eds. (West Sussex, UK: John Wiley & Sons, 2001).

failure rate: L. Fleming, "Recombinant Uncertainty in Technological Search," *Management Science* 47, special issue: *Design and Development* (2001): 117–132.

you try them: K. J. Klein and A. P. Knight, "Innovation Implementation: Overcoming the Challenge," *Current Directions in Psychological Science* 14 (2005): 243–246.

familiar ones: M. Baer, "Putting Creativity to Work: The Implementation of Creative Ideas in Organizations," *Academy of Management Journal* 55 (2012): 1102–1119.

60 *undergrad population:* J. S. Mueller, S. Melwani, and J. A. Goncalo, "The Bias against Creativity: Why People Desire but Reject Creative Ideas," *Psychological Science* 23 (2012): 13–17.

65 *to this question:* J. S. Mueller, S. Melwani, J. Loewenstein, and J. Deal, "Reframing the Decision-Makers' Dilemma: A Social Context Model of Creative Idea Recognition" (working paper).

67 *problem as well:* C. M. Ford and D. A. Gioia, "Factors Influencing Creativity in the Domain of Managerial Decision Making," *Journal of Management* 26 (2000): 705–732.

68 *economic data:* F. Ferraro, J. Pfeffer, and R. I. Sutton, "Economics Language and Assumptions: How Theories Can Become Self-Fulfilling," *Academy of Management Review* 30 (2005): 8–24.

71 *actual ability:* S. Melwani, J. S. Mueller, and J. Overbeck, "Looking Down: The Influence of Contempt and Compassion on Leadership Perceptions," *Journal of Applied Psychology* 96 (2012): 1171–1185.

4. Self-Disrupt: Overcome Your Own Bias against Creativity

73   *"21st century":* M. Chafkin, "A Broken Place: The Spectacular Failure of the Startup That Was Going to Change the World," *Fast Company,* www.fastcompany.com/3028159/a-broken-place-better -place (2014).

     merely a concept: M. Gunther, "Why a Highly Promising Electric Car Start-Up Is Failing," *Yale Environment 360,* March 5, 2013, http://e360.yale.edu/feature/gunther_why_israel_electric_car_ startup_better_place_failed/2624.

79   *and many others:* T. Fogarty, in personal communication with the author, March 2015.

83   *if you fail:* T. M. Amabile, *Creativity in Context* (Boulder, CO: Westview Press, 1996).

84   *company right now:* G. Day, "Is It Real? Can We Win? Is It Worth Doing?: Managing Risk and Reward in an Innovation Portfolio," *Harvard Business Review* 85 (2007): 110; and M. Mode, "The Post-it Note Was Introduced 35 Years Ago Today. Was It Really Invented By Mistake?," *Michael Mode,* April 6, 2015, www.magicmode.com/ the-post-it-note-introduced-35-years-ago-today-was-it-really-in-vented-by-mistake/.

85   *estimation accuracy:* J. Surowiecki, *The Wisdom of Crowds* (New York: Doubleday, 2004).

86   *novel ideas either:* J. Berg, "Balancing on the Creative High-Wire: Forecasting the Success of Novel Ideas in Organizations," *Administrative Science Quarterly* (forthcoming).

88   *the unconscious mind:* D. K. Simonton, *Origins of Genius: Darwinian Perspectives on Creativity* (New York: Oxford University Press, 1999).

     scan slightly: T. Drew, M. L.-H. Võ, and J. M. Wolfe, "The Invisible Gorilla Strikes Again: Sustained Inattentional Blindness in Expert Observers," *Psychological Science* 24 (2013): 1848–1853.

89   *simply pattern match:* T. Friend, "Tomorrow's Advance Man," *The New Yorker,* May 18, 2015, www.newyorker.com/magazine/2015 /05/18/tomorrows-advance-man.

     will move slower: J. Bargh, M. Chen, and L. Burrows, "Automaticity of Social Behavior: Direct Effects of Trait Construct and Stereotype Activation on Action," *Journal of Personality and Social Psychology* 71 (1996): 230–244.

     display poor memory: A. Dijksterhuis, J. A. Bargh, and J. Miedema, "Of Men and Mackerels: Attention, Subjective Experience, and Automatic Social Behavior," in *The Message Within: The Role of Subjective Experience in Social Cognition and Behavior* (New York: Psychology Press, 2000).

90 *cognitive biases:* A. C. Hafenbrack, Z. Kinias, and S. G. Barsade, "Debiasing the Mind through Meditation: Mindfulness and the Sunk-Cost Bias," *Psychological Science* 25 (2014): 369–376.

91 *later success:* L. Huang and J. L. Pearce, "Managing the Unknowable: The Effectiveness of Early-Stage Investor Gut Feel in Entrepreneurial Investment Decisions," *Administrative Science Quarterly* 60 (2015): 634–670.

92 *harms our health:* G. Mandler, *Mind and Body: Psychology of Emotion and Stress* (New York: W. W. Norton, 1984).

Mona Lisa: S. Lyubomirsky and S. Nolen-Hoeksema, "Self-Perpetuating Properties of Dysphoric Rumination," *Journal of Personality and Social Psychology* 65 (1993): 339–349.

93 *they also become rich:* L. Huang and J. L. Pearce, "Managing the Unknowable: The Effectiveness of Early-Stage Investor Gut Feel in Entrepreneurial Investment Decisions," *Administrative Science Quarterly* 60, no. 4 (2015): 634–670.

94 *spendthrift:* B. Schlender and R. Tetzeli, *Becoming Steve Jobs: The Evolution of a Reckless Upstart into a Visionary Leader* (New York: Crown Business, 2015).

95 *social acceptance:* J. Loewenstein and J. S. Mueller, "Implicit Theories of Creative Ideas: How Culture Shapes Assessments of Creative Ideas," *Academy of Management Discoveries* (forthcoming).

less feasible it is: E. Rietzschel, B. Nijstad, and W. Stroebe, "The Selection of Creative Ideas after Individual Idea Generation: Choosing between Creativity and Impact," *British Journal of Psychology* 101 (2010): 47–68.

96 *higher-quality creative solutions:* C. P. Moreau and D. W. Dahl, "Designing the Solution: The Impact of Constraints on Consumers' Creativity," *Journal of Consumer Research* 32 (2005): 13–22; R. Y.-J. Chua and S. S. Iyengar, "Creativity as a Matter of Choice: Prior Experience and Task Instruction as Boundary Conditions for the Positive Effect of Choice on Creativity," *Journal of Creative Behavior* 42 (2008): 164–180; and J. A. Goncalo, J. Chatman, M. Duguid, and J. A. Kennedy, "Creativity from Constraint? How Political Correctness Influences Creativity in Mixed-Sex Work

Groups," *Administrative Science Quarterly,* vol. 60, no. 1 (2015): 1–30.

99 *providing their answers:* J. A. Minson, J. S. Mueller, and R. P. Larrick (working paper).

"could it be?": http://news.fintech.io/post/102cskz/the-new-yorker-on-marc-andreessen-and-his-plan-to-win-the-future.

5. Overcome Others' Bias against Creativity

103 *than the new:* S. Eidelman, C. S. Crandall, and J. Pattershall, "The Existence Bias," *Journal of Personality and Social Psychology* 97 (2009): 765–775.

others are doing: R. B. Cialdini, "Crafting Normative Messages to Protect the Environment," *Current Directions in Psychological Science* 12.4 (2003): 105–109; and M. M. Duguid and M. C. Thomas-Hunt, "Condoning Stereotyping? How Awareness of Stereotyping Prevalence Impacts Expression of Stereotypes," *Journal of Applied Psychology* 100, no. 2 (2015): 343.

105 *an Apple logo:* G. M. Fitzsimons, T. L. Chartrand, and G. J. Fitzsimons, "Automatic Effects of Brand Exposure on Motivated Behavior: How Apple Makes You 'Think Different,'" *Journal of Consumer Research* 35 (2008): 21–35.

one journalist: C. Chase, "Bob Dylan's Bizarre New Commercial with IBM's Watson," *USA Today,* October 6, 2015, http://ftw.usa today.com/2015/10/bob-dylan-ibm-watson-commercial.

108 *product is creative:* J. Loewenstein and J. S. Mueller, "Implicit Theories of Creative Ideas: How Culture Shapes Assessments of Creative Ideas," *Academy of Management Discoveries* (forthcoming).

109 *"poster boy?":* W. Isaacson, *Einstein: His Life and Universe* (New York: Simon & Schuster, 2007).

111 *message or angst:* D. Pollock, *Skywalking: The Life and Films of George Lucas* (New York: Da Capo Press, 1999).

115 *produce creative ideas:* M. A. Cronin and J. Loewenstein, *The Craft of Creativity* (Stanford University Press, in development).

117 *affect and creativity link:* T. M. Amabile, S. G. Barsade, J. S. Mueller, and B. M. Staw, "Affect and Creativity at Work," *Administrative Science Quarterly* 50 (2005): 367–403.

123 *Journalist profiled AO+:* J. Scott, "My No-Soap, No-Shampoo, Bacteria-Rich Hygiene Experiment," *New York Times Magazine,*

May 22, 2014, www.nytimes.com/2014/05/25/magazine/my-no-soap-no-shampoo-bacteria-rich-hygiene-experiment.html?_r=0.

most-emailed list: J. Berger and K. L. Milkman, "What makes online content viral?," *Journal of Marketing Research* 49 (2012): 192–205.

126 *use our ideas:* C. Heath and D. Heath, *Made to Stick: Why Some Ideas Survive and Others Die* (New York: Random House, 2007).

127 *likely to succeed:* M. A. Runco and R. E. Charles, "Judgments of Originality and Appropriateness as Predictors of Creativity," *Personality and Individual Differences* 15 (1993): 537–546; and P. J. Silvia, "Discernment and Creativity: How Well Can People Identify Their Most Creative Ideas?," *Psychology of Aesthetics, Creativity, and the Arts* 2 (2008): 139.

128 *strong creative potential:* K. D. Elsbach and R. M. Kramer, "Assessing Creativity in Hollywood Pitch Meetings: Evidence for a Dual-Process Model of Creativity Judgments," *Academy of Management Journal* 46 (2003): 283–301.

129 *generate creative ideas:* J. S. Mueller and D. Kamdar, "Why Seeking Help from Teammates Is a Blessing and a Curse: A Theory of Help Seeking and Individual Creativity in Team Contexts," *Journal of Applied Psychology* 96 (2011): 263–276.

those who don't: A. S. Rosette, J. S. Mueller, and R. D. Lebel, "Are Male Leaders Penalized for Seeking Help? The Influence of Gender and Asking Behaviors on Competence Perceptions," *Leadership Quarterly* 26, no. 5 (2015): 749–762.

132 *relative to novices:* C. P. Moreau, D. R. Lehmann, and A. B. Markman, "Entrenched Knowledge Structures and Consumer Response to New Products," *Journal of Marketing Research* 38, no. 1 (2001): 14–29.

6. Cultivating Creative Change in Your Organization

137 *pivot the company:* M. Freeman, "Qualcomm CEO: 'We have to pivot the company,'" *San Diego Union Tribune,* September 2, 2015, www.sandiegouniontribune.com/news/2015/sep/02/qualcomm-ceo-pivot-the-company.

138 *innovation prowess:* D. Steinbock, *The Nokia Revolution: The Story of an Extraordinary Company That Transformed an Industry* (New York: AMACOM, 2001); and K. Dittrich and G. Duys-

ters, "Networking as a Means to Strategy Change: The Case of Open Innovation in Mobile Telephony," *Journal of Product Innovation Management* 24, no. 6 (2007): 510–521.

a nimble Finnish company: J. Surowiecki, "Where Nokia Went Wrong," *The New Yorker,* September 3, 2013, www.newyorker.com/business/currency/where-nokia-went-wrong.

autonomy to workers: T. M. Amabile, et al., "Assessing the Work Environment for Creativity," *Academy of Management Journal* 39, no. 5 (1996): 1154–1184; and S. G. Scott and R. A. Bruce, "Determinants of Innovative Behavior: A Path Model of Individual Innovation in the Workplace," *Academy of Management Journal* 37, no. 3 (1994): 580–607.

139 *possibly ostracized:* M. J. Gelfand, et al., "Differences between Tight and Loose Cultures: A 33-Nation Study," *Science* 332, no. 6033 (May 2011): 1100–1104.

company to adhere to: R. Katz and T. J. Allen, "Investigating the Not Invented Here (NIH) Syndrome: A Look at the Performance, Tenure, and Communication Patterns of 50 R&D Project Groups," *R&D Management,* 12, no. 1 (1982): 7.

141 *organizational hierarchy:* C. B. Gibson, et al., Hierarchical Perceptual Distance: A New Perspective on the Relationship between Perception Differences and Business Performance (working paper, University of Western Australia).

143 *"to these students?":* C. Pazzanese, "'I had this extraordinary sense of liberation': Nitin Nohria's Exhilarating Journey," *Harvard Gazette,* April 29, 2015.

144 *"it will be better":* J. Byrne, "HBS Dean Makes an Unusual Public Apology," *Poets & Quants,* January 28, 2014.

145 *confirms their beliefs:* R. S. Nickerson, "Confirmation Bias: A Ubiquitous Phenomenon in Many Guises," *Review of General Psychology* 2 (1998): 175–220.

going to buy it: P. R. Nayak and J. M. Ketteringham, *Breakthroughs!* (New York: Rawson Associates, 1986).

146 *"complete addiction":* M. Mode, "The Post-it Note Was Introduced 35 Years Ago Today. Was It Really Invented By Mistake?," *Michael Mode,* April 6, 2015, www.magicmode.com/the-post-it-note-introduced-35-years-ago-today-was-it-really-invented-by-mistake/.

148 *dependence upon oil?:* www.ted.com/talks/shai_agassi_on_electric_cars/transcript?language=en.

225

149   *chronicled a mystery:* J. Bussey, "The Innovator's Enigma," *Wall Street Journal,* October 4, 2012, www.wsj.com/articles/SB10000872 396390443493304578036753351798378.

     "changed them": M. Gladwell, "The Tweaker: The Real Genius of Steve Jobs," *The New Yorker,* November 14, 2011, www.newyorker.com/magazine/2011/11/14/the-tweaker.

     "socially horrifying": M. Gladwell, "How David Beats Goliath" When Underdogs Break the Rules," *The New Yorker,* May 11, 2009, www.newyorker.com/magazine/2009/05/11/how-david-beats-goliath.

     Picasso of our generation: S. Rosenbaum, "Steve Jobs Wasn't the Einstein of Our Generation, He Was the Picasso," *Fast Company,* November 9, 2011, www.fastcompany.com/1793428/steve-jobs-wasnt-einstein-our-generation-he-was-picasso.

151   *emotional conflict:* C.K.W. De Dreu and L. R. Weingart, "Task versus Relationship Conflict, Team Performance, and Team Member Satisfaction: A Meta-Analysis." *Journal of Applied Psychology* 88, no. 4 (2003): 741–749.

152   *expressing a new idea:* M. Diehl and W. Stroebe, "Productivity Loss in Brainstorming Groups: Toward the Solution of a Riddle," *Journal of Personality and Social Psychology* 53, no. 3 (1987): 497–509; and M. Diehl and W. Stroebe, "Productivity Loss in Idea-Generating Groups: Tracking Down the Blocking Effect," *Journal of Personality and Social Psychology* 61, no. 3 (1991): 392–403.

156   *manage innovation:* R. Cooper, "Managing Technology Development Projects," *Research Technology Management* 49, no. 6 (2006): 23.

158   *in the long term:* C. M. Ford and D. A. Gioia, "Factors Influencing Creativity in the Domain of Managerial Decision Making," *Journal of Management* 26, no. 4 (2000): 705–732.

161   *"it's theoretical?":* John Walker interview, *The Incredibles,* DVD, directed by Brad Bird (Burbank, CA: Walt Disney Home Entertainment, 2005).

     creative new products: R. Cook, in personal communication with the author, January 2016.

7. Overcome the Bias against Creative Leadership

167   *wins decades:* B. Brown, S. Anthony, "How P&G Tripled Its Innovation Success Rate," *Harvard Business Review* (June 2011).

McDonald's leadership: J. Bogaisky, "Congrats, Bill Ackman: Bob McDonald Out at P&G, A. G. Lafley Returning as CEO," *Forbes,* May 2013.

"innovation guru": J. Surowiecki, "The Comeback Conundrum," *The New Yorker,* September 21, 2015.

Jobs to Apple: J. Green, "P&G Looks for Steve Jobs–Like Sequel by Recalling Ex-CEO," *Bloomberg Businessweek,* May 25, 2013, www.bloomberg.com/news/articles/2013-05-24/p-g-looks-for-steve -jobs-like-sequel-by-recalling-ex-ceo.

168 *underperformed the market:* J. Surowiecki, "The Comeback Co-nundrum," *The New Yorker,* September 21, 2015.

win in the future: F. Kern, "What Chief Executives Really Want," *Bloomberg Businessweek,* May 17, 2010, www.bloomberg.com /news/articles/2010-05-18/what-chief-executives-really-want.

replied, "curiosity": "A Marketplace without Boundaries? Responding to Disruption," www.pwc.com/gx/en/ceo-survey/2015/ assets/pwc-18th-annual-global-ceo-survey-jan-2015.pdf.

prove the concept: T. Wedell-Wedellsborg, "What It Really Means to Be a Chief Innovation Officer," *Harvard Business Review,* December 2014, https://hbr.org/2014/12/what-it-really-means-to-be-a -chief-innovation-officer.

innovation and creativity: P. Kannan-Narasimhan, "Organizational Ingenuity in Nascent Innovations: Gaining Resources and Legitimacy through Unconventional Actions," *Organization Studies* 35 (2014): 483–509.

169 *and interesting:* K. D. Elsbach, R. M. Kramer, "Assessing Creativity in Hollywood Pitch Meetings: Evidence for a Dual-Process Model of Creativity Judgments," *Academy of Management Journal* 46 (2003): 283–301; and R. J. Sternberg, "Implicit Theories of Intelligence, Creativity, and Wisdom," *Journal of Personality and Social Psychology* 49 (1985): 607–627.

170 *at important tasks:* S. Taggar, R. Hackett, and S. Saha, "Leadership Emergence in Autonomous Work Teams: Antecedents and Outcomes," *Personnel Psychology* 52 (1999): 899–926.

employing stereotypes: R. G. Lord, R. J. Foti, and C. L. de Vader, "A Test of Leadership Categorization Theory: Internal Structure, Information Processing, and Leadership Perceptions," *Organizational Behavior & Human Performance* 34 (1984): 343–378; and J. R. Meindl, S. B. Ehrlich, and J. M. Dukerich, "The Romance of Leadership," *Administrative Science Quarterly* 30 (1985): 78–102.

and attractive: A. S. Rosette, G. J. Leonardelli, and K. W. Phillips, "The White Standard: Racial Bias in Leader Categorization," *Journal of Applied Psychology* 93 (2008): 758–777; and L. R. Offermann, J. K. Kennedy, and P. W. Wirtz, "Implicit Leadership Theories: Content, Structure, and Generalizability," *Leadership Quarterly* 5 (1994): 43–58.

fit all the criteria: A. S. Rosette, J. S. Mueller, and R. D. Lebel, "Are Male Leaders Penalized for Seeking Help? The Influence of Gender and Asking Behaviors on Competence Perceptions," *Leadership Quarterly* 26 (2015): 749–762.

171   *to be leaderlike:* J. S. Mueller, J. A. Goncalo, and D. Kamdar, "Recognizing Creative Leadership: Can Creative Idea Expression Negatively Relate to Perceptions of Leadership Potential?," *Journal of Experimental Social Psychology* 47 (2011): 494–498.

172   *ultimately fails:* S. R. Giessner and D. van Knippenberg, "'License to Fail': Goal Definition, Leader Group Prototypicality, and Perceptions of Leadership Effectiveness After Leader Failure," *Organizational Behavior and Human Decision Processes* 105 (2008): 14–35.

173   *promotes effective leadership:* D. Vera, A. Rodriguez-Lopez, "Strategic Virtues: Humility as a Source of Competitive Advantage," in "Healthy, Happy, Productive Work: A Leadership Challenge," special issue, *Organizational Dynamics* 33 (2004): 393–408; B. P. Owens and D. R. Hekman, "Modeling How to Grow: An Inductive Examination of Humble Leader Behaviors, Contingencies, and Outcomes," *Academy of Management Journal* 55 (2012): 787–818; D. Van Dierendonck, "Servant Leadership: A Review and Synthesis," *Journal of Management* 37 (2011): 1228–1261; and B. J. Avolio, F. O. Walumbwa, and T. J. Weber, "Leadership: Current Theories, Research, and Future Directions," *Annual Review of Psychology* 60 (2009): 421–449.

and employees: J. Pfeffer, *Leadership BS: Fixing Workplaces and Careers One Truth at a Time* (New York: HarperBusiness, 2015).

through twelfth grade: K. H. Kim, "The Creativity Crisis: The Decrease in Creative Thinking Scores on the Torrance Tests of Creative Thinking," *Creativity Research Journal* 23 (2011): 285–295.

arts, like dance: K. Robinson, (2006, February). Ken Robinson: Do schools kill creativity? (video file). Retrieved from www.ted.com/talks/ken_robinson_says_schools_kill_creativity.

is not essential: A. Andiliou and P. K. Murphy, "Examining Variations Among Researchers' and Teachers' Conceptualizations of Creativity: A Review and Synthesis of Contemporary Research," *Educational Research Review* 5 (2010): 201–219.

176 *4 percent per year:* D. Munro, "U.S. Healthcare Hits $3 Trillion," *Forbes,* January 9, 2012, www.forbes.com/sites/danmunro /2012/01/19/u-s-healthcare-hits-3-trillion/#69b0f2e72f67.

181 *feel more confident:* C. Anderson, S. Brion, D. A. Moore, and J. A. Kennedy, "A Status-Enhancement Account of Overconfidence," *Journal of Personality and Social Psychology* 103 (2012): 718–735; and D. R. Carney, A. J. C. Cuddy, and A. J. Yap, "Power Posing: Brief Nonverbal Displays Affect Neuroendocrine Levels and Risk Tolerance," *Psychological Science* 21, no. 10 (2010): 1363–1368.

performance goes down: J. K. Maner and N. L. Mead, "The Essential Tension Between Leadership and Power: When Leaders Sacrifice Group Goals for the Sake of Self-Interest," *Journal of Personality and Social Psychology* 99 (2010): 482.

183 *during decision making:* D. J. Isenberg, "Group Polarization: A Critical Review and Meta-Analysis," *Journal of Personality and Social Psychology* 50 (1986): 1141–1151.

189 *"very tight loop":* K. Greenfeld, *Wall Street Journal,* "How Mark Parker Keeps Nike in the Lead," *Wall Street Journal,* November 4, 2015, www.wsj.com/articles/how-mark-parker-keeps-nike-in -the-lead-1446689666.

"the research side": A. Ignatius and D. McGinn, "Novo Nordisk CEO Lars Sorensen on What Propelled Him to the Top," *Harvard Business Review,* November 2015, https://hbr.org/2015/11/novo -nordisk-ceo-on-what-propelled-him-to-the-top.

8. Stop Generating Ideas and Start Making Impact

193 *more ideas:* D. K. Simonton, "Scientific Creativity as Constrained Stochastic Behavior: The Integration of Product, Person, and Process Perspectives," *Psychological Bulletin* 129 (2003): 475–494.

high quality: K. Girotra, C. Terwiesch, and K. T. Ulrich, "Idea Generation and the Quality of the Best Idea," *Management Science* 56 (2010): 591–605.

194 *to choose from:* E. Ries, *The Lean Startup: How Today's Entrepre-*

229

neurs Use Continuous Innovation to Create Radically Successful Businesses (New York: Random House, 2011).

ten a penny: M. A. West, "Ideas Are Ten a Penny: It's Team Implementation Not Idea Generation That Counts," *Applied Psychology: An International Review* 51 (2002): 411–424.

status quo increases: A. Kempf and S. Ruenzi, "Status Quo Bias and the Number of Alternatives: An Empirical Illustration from the Mutual Fund Industry," *Journal of Behavioral Finance* 7 (2006): 204–213; and W. Samuelson and R. Zeckhauser, "Status Quo Bias in Decision Making," *Journal of Risk and Uncertainty* 1 (1988): 7–59.

options decreases: P. Criscuolo, L. Dahlander, T. Grohsjean, and A. Salter, "Evaluating Novelty: The Role of Panels in the Selection of R&D Projects," *Academy of Management Journal,* March 8, 2016, amj.2014.0861.

200 *"in the market":* T. M. Amabile and M. Khaire, "Creativity and the Role of the Leader," *Harvard Business Review,* October 2008, https://hbr.org/2008/10/creativity-and-the-role-of-the-leader.

202 *"do this job":* J. Howell, "The Right Stuff: Identifying and Developing Effective Champions of Innovation," *Academy of Management Executive* 19 (2005): 108–119.

205 *around five people:* R.I.M. Dunbar, N.D.C. Duncan, and D. Nettle, "Size and Structure of Freely Forming Conversational Groups," *Human Nature* 6 (1995): 67–78.

206 *answer is often no:* E. Miron-Spektor, M. Erez, and E. Naveh, "The Effect of Conformist and Attentive-to-Detail Members on Team Innovation: Reconciling the Innovation Paradox," *Academy of Management Journal* 54 (2011): 740–760.

arm of a company: D. G. Ancona, "Outward Bound: Strategies for Team Survival in an Organization," *Academy of Management Journal* 33 (1990): 334–365; and D. G. Ancona and D. F. Caldwell, "Bridging the Boundary: External Activity and Performance in Organizational Teams," *Administrative Science Quarterly* 37 (1992): 634–665.

207 *in the room:* Brad Power, "Improve Decision-Making with Help from the Crowd," *Harvard Business Review,* April 8, 2014.

210 *"everything wrong":* B. M. Staw, "Why No One Really Wants Creativity," in *Creative Action in Organizations: Ivory Tower Visions and Real World Voices,* C. Ford, D. A. Gioia, eds. (Thousand Oaks, CA: Sage Publications, 1995).

Index